Corporate Law, Codes of Conduct and Workers' Rights

This book critically explores how increased regulation and governance of corporations can be used to help improve the rights of workers amidst an era of union decline.

The book posits that soft law techniques such as codes of conduct are more effective in protecting workers than "hard law," i.e. domestic regulation. It starts by analysing the transnational regulation of corporations and codes of conduct, and then puts forward a model code of conduct that can be used by corporations to help increase the protection of workers. Through this model's use of a monitoring scheme, shareholders, activists, and NGOs put pressure on the corporation to reform itself and enact a code which has obligations flowing both ways between the corporation and its employees. The book then looks at the expansions of fiduciary duties and changes to corporate governance, including Benefit Corporations and how they can be used to increase the rights of workers. It then discusses changes to standard union contracts before concluding with an assessment of the best way forward for workers' rights.

By providing a new contribution to the current dialogue on corporate social responsibility and codes of conduct, this book will be a valuable resource for academics working on labour, employment, and business law as well as corporate lawyers.

Vanisha H. Sukdeo is a Course Instructor of Law at Osgoode Hall Law School, York University, Canada.

Routledge Research in Corporate Law

Available titles in this series include

Corporate Law and Financial Instability
Andreas Kokkinis

Behavioural Risks in Corporate Governance
Regulatory Intervention as a Risk Management Mechanism
Ngozi Vivian Okoye

Indonesian Company Law
Soonpeel Edgar Chang

Regulation and Inequality at Work
Isolation and Inequality Beyond the Regulation of Labour
Vanisha Sukdeo

Regulation and the Credit Rating Agencies
Restraining Ancillary Services
Daniel Cash

Law and Responsible Supply Chain Management
Contract and Tort Interplay and Overlap
Edited by Vibe Ulfbeck, Alexandra Andhov and Kateřina Mitkidis

Shareholder Primacy and Global Business
Re-clothing the EU Corporate Law
Lela Mélon

Corporate Law, Codes of Conduct and Workers' Rights
Vanisha H. Sukdeo

Corporate Law, Codes of Conduct and Workers' Rights

Vanisha H. Sukdeo

Routledge
Taylor & Francis Group
LONDON AND NEW YORK

First published 2020
by Routledge
2 Park Square, Milton Park, Abingdon, Oxon OX14 4RN

and by Routledge
605 Third Avenue, New York, NY 10017

First issued in paperback 2021

Routledge is an imprint of the Taylor & Francis Group, an informa business

Publisher's Note
The publisher has gone to great lengths to ensure the quality of this reprint but points out that some imperfections in the original copies may be apparent.

British Library Cataloguing-in-Publication Data
A catalogue record for this book is available from the British Library

Library of Congress Cataloging-in-Publication Data
Names: Sukdeo, Vanisha H., 1981– author.
Title: Corporate law, codes of conduct and workers' rights / Vanisha Sukdeo.
Description: Abingdon, Oxon ; New York, NY : Routledge, 2019. | Series: Routledge research in corporate law | Includes bibliographical references and index.
Identifiers: LCCN 2019010620 (print) | LCCN 2019017501 (ebook) | ISBN 9780429059889 (ebk) | ISBN 9780367181727 (hbk)
Subjects: LCSH: Labor laws and legislation. | Social responsibility of business—Law and legislation. | Corporate governance—Law and legislation. | Labor laws and legislation.—Canada. | Social responsibility of business—Law and legislation—Canada. | Corporate governance—Law and legislation—Canada.
Classification: LCC K1715 (ebook) | LCC K1715 .S85 2019 (print) | DDC 344.01—dc23
LC record available at https://lccn.loc.gov/2019010620

ISBN 13: 978-1-03-224101-2 (pbk)
ISBN 13: 978-0-367-18172-7 (hbk)

DOI: 10.4324/9780429059889

Typeset in Galliard
by Apex CoVantage, LLC

Contents

Tables

Textboxes

Acknowledgements

I would like to thank Emma Tyce and the Routledge staff for accepting my book. Emma's help and support in getting my work to completion has been greatly appreciated. The support and guidance I have received from Routledge has been more than expected. I truly value the time and effort of everyone who is a part of bringing my book to production.

Thank you to my mother and sister. I would also like to thank my friends who have endured my talking about the promise of corporate codes of conduct.

Thank you to my former students, who make me proud of their accomplishments, and their ongoing thirst for knowledge.

Thank you to the reviewers of the book proposal, who enabled me to create a better product than I envisioned at the early stages.

What made me write this book was my drive to help workers find their voice in their own workplaces and how those workplaces are governed. How much autonomy is given to workers during the course of performing work? To have one's voice not merely heard but acknowledged and included is the goal of my research.

Overview of the book

This book critically explores how the increased regulation and governance of corporations can be used to help improve the rights of workers. Chapter 1 outlines the introduction and background. Chapter 2 explores transnational regulation of corporations and codes of conduct, and it offers a Model Code of Conduct that can be used by corporations to help increase the protections for workers. Chapter 3 looks at the expansions of fiduciary duties and changes to corporate governance and how it can be used to increase the rights of workers, and Chapter 4 looks at changes to standard union contracts. Chapter 5 is the concluding chapter.

This book examines The interconnections between corporate governance and the rights of workers by exploring codes of conduct. After the examination of several codes I devise a model code of conduct to be used by corporations to function in line with CSR that allows for greater reach. I ground my research in corporate law as the internal mechanism of the code allows for internal change.

Codes of conduct that concern increasing or strengthening the rights of workers can fit under the broader umbrella of CSR. The term CSR is used to differentiate from the alternate model of corporations existing solely for their shareholders and to increase profit, and it means that corporations have duties to other stakeholders beyond shareholders.[1] Those stakeholders include, but are not limited to, employees and those who produce goods and provide services,[2] the environmental agencies and government. This book will also examine the differences in how "soft law"[3] and "hard law"[4] can be used to help develop the rights of workers.

1 See later for a further discussion about shareholder primacy model versus stakeholder theory.

2 Sometimes those who produce goods and services for a certain company may not be "employees" of that company but still have rights and obligations that flow from such a relationship even though it may not be termed "an employment relationship."

3 "Soft law" can be defined as the use of codes of conduct, governmental norms, voluntary standards, and the work of advocacy groups and other stakeholders in shaping the responsibilities of corporations.

4 The term "hard law" is used to describe legislation and legally binding agreements.

Author biography

Vanisha H. Sukdeo is a Ph.D. candidate at Osgoode Hall Law School in Toronto, Ontario, Canada. Vanisha currently works as a Course Instructor at Osgoode Hall Law School. Vanisha was called to the Ontario Bar in 2007 after completing her articles with Ryder Wright Blair & Holmes LLP, and the Ontario Public Service Employees Union (OPSEU). She received her LL.M. from Osgoode, her LL.B. from Queen's University, and her Bachelor of Arts from York University where she majored in political science. Vanisha taught at Osgoode Hall as a Course Director for five years before becoming an Adjunct Professor at Western Law. In 2012 Vanisha was a nominee for the Ian Greene Award for Teaching Excellence, which is a University-wide teaching award.

Vanisha's first book with Routledge was entitled *Regulation and Inequality at Work: Isolation and Inequality beyond the Regulation of Labour* and published in July 2018.

Her email address is: VSukdeo@osgoode.yorku.ca

1 Introduction

This book critically explores how the increased regulation and governance of corporations can be used to help improve the rights of workers. Chapter 1 outlines the introduction and literature review, Chapter 2 explores transnational regulation of corporations and codes of conduct, Chapter 3 looks at the expansions of fiduciary duties and changes to corporate governance and how it can be used to increase the rights of workers, and Chapter 4 looks at changes to standard union contracts. Chapter 5 is the concluding chapter. My original contribution is looking at how labour law and corporate governance rarely intersect. But at this important intersection, there lies the promise for workers. By using CSR, and ethical consumption, the worker is able to gain increased rights.

Background of the problem

My study is situated within a broader debate about CSR (Dirk Matten and Andrew Crane), codes of conduct (Rhys Jenkins and Richard Locke), and increasing workers' rights outside of hard law (Archon Fung, Dara O'Rourke, and Charles Sabel). When the sweatshop free movement started, certain companies branded themselves as sweatshop free in order to build their consumer base. Companies like American Apparel built their image as sweatshop free clothing manufacturers. Other companies such as the Gap changed their policies in regards to sweatshops due to external pressure from unions such as UNITE HERE.[1] My research investigates how to use corporate law in such a way that would increase the rights of workers. This research will analyse whether it is possible to build corporations that are socially responsible and that can improve the rights of workers, as the two are not mutually exclusive. My focus will be on how codes of conduct act as a soft law mechanism to implement change.

1 See work of UNITE HERE in regards to getting media attention about the Gap and its use of sweatshops. Maquila Solidarity Network: http://en.maquilasolidarity.org/resources/video/StopSweatshops.

Purpose of the study

This study will be useful in crafting new solutions to existing problems about the divide between soft law and hard law. This research pushes beyond the law into the business, management, and industrial relations disciplines. This research may also be of use in the environmental studies area, as the corporate social responsibility umbrella covers the environmental effects caused by corporations.

Corporations may promote CSR initiatives in order to satisfy external pressures but may fail to do anything specific to adequately build social responsibility. Corporations may also brand themselves as socially responsible in recognition of the shift to ethical consumption. "Ethical consumption refers to retail customers' opting for goods that are perceived to create more preferable social economic or environmental impacts and outcomes than competing equivalent."[2] This may force corporations to put substance behind their claims to be socially responsible. Because consumers are becoming more knowledgeable about products, the demand for ethical products may put pressure on corporations to make its products ethical.

Codes of conduct and ethical consumption are linked in that consumer pressure for more ethical products may force corporations to adopt a code of conduct. Professor Compa states that "[t]oday a new generation of codes called 'multi-stakeholder' initiatives has appeared. Companies, unions, human rights groups, community and development organizations, and other NGOs participate in formulating a code of conduct."[3] He argues that corporate social responsibility is most effective when used alongside strong legislation and trade unions where workers are able to freely bargain and are able to effect change.[4] This statement will be examined as his notion of unions working in conjunction with the corporation to bring about a CSR enlightened code of conduct is fascinating.

In this book I look at how corporate governance mechanisms be used to help increase the rights of workers. I also look at whether codes of conduct are a useful tool to use in order to strengthen the rights of workers. My hypothesis is that, while corporate governance mechanisms such as codes of conduct may be effective tools in strengthening the rights of workers, they are but a few tools among many available, and that many tools being used at the same time for the same purpose will prove more effective than a single tool.

2 Wayne Visser et al., *The A to Z of Corporate Social Responsibility: A Complete Guide to Concepts, Codes and Organisations* (West Sussex: John Wiley & Sons Ltd, 2007), at 195.

3 Lance Compa, "Corporate Social Responsibility and Workers' Rights" online: <http://digitalcommons.ilr.cornell.edu/articles/183/>, at 5.

4 Lance Compa, "Corporate Social Responsibility and Workers' Rights" online: <http://digitalcommons.ilr.cornell.edu/articles/183/>, at 6.

Theoretical framework

My study is situated within a broader debate about corporate social responsibility that also includes the debates about workers' rights and supply chains more broadly. The debate about CSR can be traced to the Berle and Dodd debates in 1931, where the issue of who managers actually serve was raised – is the obligation owed to shareholders? Or to some other group? Both American and Canadian corporate law is shareholder-centric, where shareholder primacy model/shareholder wealth maximization is still the theory that is enforced. Obviously, Supreme Court of Canada decisions such as *BCE* have made changes to the law that requires Directors to "consider interests" of stakeholders beyond shareholders, but the extent of this obligation is still unclear. As well, the term CSR is still relatively new, and a definite definition is not agreed upon. Even the notion of corporate philanthropy and whether this falls under CSR is being debated; as if the assertion that shareholders are the owners of the corporation stands, then according to agency theory, the Directors and officers of a corporation have an obligation to focus on shareholder wealth and giving away the corporation's money is running afoul of agency theory. Scholars such as Donaldson, Drucker, and Jensen have varying theories about CSR, where no one theory is held to be definitive and absolute. CSR can be critiqued from the left as being mere whitewashing and ineffective. It can also be used by corporations to stave off actual state regulation in place of private or self-regulation. CSR can be critiqued from the right as being beyond the scope of the corporation. If the corporation operates with a view to a profit, it can be held that social obligations fall outside the true mandate of the corporation. If the corporation was intended from creation to be socially oriented, then the applicable legislation would reflect the same. The fact that other corporate forms like the Benefit Corporation exist echoes the refrain that the "original" corporate form was not meant to be socially oriented because the need for these new forms reflect CSR, not the "original" form of the corporation. If all corporations were meant to be CSR corporations, then Benefit Corporations would never have been created because they would serve no purpose. Milton Friedman argues that businesses have no obligations beyond avoiding fraud and deception, but this statement is antiquated and no longer applicable. Due to recent corporate law decisions in Canada, we see the SCC shift towards greater corporate accountability and transparency. These shifts have resulted in a change to the corporate form as it existed years ago when Friedman wrote. Even if the past corporation did not have to be socially responsible, the modern-day corporation has to be reformed to reflect the changing values of both society and the actual caselaw in Canada.

Corporate governance theory can be traced back to Ronald Coase and his article "The Nature of the Firm," and to Michael Jensen and his writings on agency theory. Adolf A. Berle published "For Whom Corporate Managers Are Trustees: A Note" in 1932 to continue the debate with Dodd over the obligations of Directors. Milton Friedman in 1970 declared that corporations do not have social responsibilities, as the responsibilities of businesses was to merely increase profit and avoid doing so by deception and fraud. R. Edward Freeman devised stakeholder theory, which is still held up in opposition to shareholder primacy model/shareholder wealth maximization. The differing views of corporate governance can be ascribed to Lynn Stout's work on stakeholder theory, and Henry Hansmann and Reinier Kraakman in "What Is Corporate Law?"

Theory of the firm – how does the corporation function?

Note that the question is framed as to how the corporation functions rather than how the corporation *should* function. The question of how the corporation should function is more open to interpretation than that of how it functions, in that one's beliefs and value system will influence how one determines the best way for the corporation to aspire to act.

Ronald Coase

"The Nature of the Firm"[5] by Ronald Coase is a fundamental article in economics because Coase sets out to explain why an individual would choose to join a firm (partnership, corporation, or other entity) rather than work independently as an entrepreneur. "[I]f some people preferred to work under the direction of some other person. Such individuals would accept less in order to work under someone, and firms would arise naturally from this."[6] This seems to be about shifting liability in that an individual as sole proprietor would have full responsibility, while as simply a member of a firm, the individual is able to shift or spread liability. Coase does not address this issue which may be more of a legal issue than an economic one. Coase argues that by allowing individuals to share resources and restrict transactions to internal ones rather than external, prices decrease. Also, he notes that there is less interaction with the outside market by keeping services within the firm.

One reason people choose to join partnerships, besides the ability to spread liability to others, is the tax advantages of being a partner over an associate. This is in the law firm context, but there are tax advantages to working with others rather than independently, as corporations are taxed differently from individuals. "If we consider the operation of a sales tax, it is clear that it is a tax on market transactions and not on the same transactions organized within the firm."[7] About the price benefits to operating a firm over market transactions, one need not look further than in-house counsel versus hiring a lawyer in private practice. There are advantages to having someone within the organization do

5 Ronald Coase, "The Nature of the Firm" *Economica* vol 4 no 16 (Nov. 1937) pp. 386–405.

6 Ronald Coase, "The Nature of the Firm" *Economica* vol 4 no 16 (Nov. 1937) pp. 386–405 at 390.

7 Ronald Coase, "The Nature of the Firm" *Economica* vol 4 no 16 (Nov. 1937) pp. 386–405 at 393.

the work rather than hiring someone in private practice. Not only is the concern about money, but various other factors lead one to conclude that in-house has benefits over contracting out. First, the employer would expect that someone who works for the organization would have a sense of loyalty above someone who works in private practice and handles numerous cases. Second, it is often required that someone doing work for an organization has knowledge about the workplaces that are being discussed, and someone who works at the organization full-time is more likely to have a greater understanding of the organization's workings and members than someone who is in private practice.

Coase asserts that a firm will increase to use the advantage to the fullest:

> Other things being equal, therefore, a firm will tend to be larger: a) the less the costs of organizing and the slower these costs rise with an increase in the transactions organized. b) the less likely the entrepreneur is to make mistakes and the smaller the increase in mistakes with an increase in the transactions organized. c) the greater the lowering (or the less the rise) in the supply price of factors of production to firms of larger size.[8]

This explains why multinational corporations keep growing: they are able to have transactions take place between company headquarters rather than have to do business in the broader market. The area of transfer pricing also explains how firms and corporations are able to use tax incentives to their advantage.

Other theorists beyond Coase postulate that the corporation is a nexus of contracts or that the Directors and Officers of the corporation are mere agents for the shareholders. Jensen's agency theory would determine that shareholder wealth maximization is the driving force of the corporation and, in the words of Milton Friedman, "the business of business is business" to the exclusion of other stakeholders. The nexus of contracts theory claims that the corporation is merely a nexus of differing contracts, such as the contract between the corporation and its bondholders, and the corporation and its employees, etc. Those excluded from the contract model are left without recourse. This model very much grounds corporate law in contract law.

Nexus of contracts

The nexus of contracts theory postulates that the corporation is merely the epicenter through which other contracts flow. Contracts merely intersect and intermingle at the site of the corporation.

Keep in mind that shareholders do not have a contract with the corporation yet occupy a revered position. "Some argue that shareholders are the real risk-takers in a corporate nexus, and as such, they are the engines of innovation,

8 Ronald Coase, "The Nature of the Firm" *Economica* vol 4 no 16 (Nov. 1937) pp. 386–405 at 397.

growth and capitalism."[9] While this may hold true for shareholders who invest in startup businesses and other risky ventures, the same cannot be said about someone who decides to buy shares in Microsoft or Apple or Bell – those are strong shares that are pretty secure. This idea that a shareholder swoops in to give money to a new company to jolt it into existence or fund some new innovation is not true across the board. Professors Zumbansen and Archer note that

> Commentators such as Professor MacIntosh rejected the QCA (and Wise) decision, recognizing in the QCA's approach nothing but a misunderstanding of the "true" theory of the firm. The firm, he and they suggest, is much more like a "nexus of contracts," within which the bondholders are themselves one type of contractor.[10]

Nexus of contracts acts to lower all participants to the same level and mask the inequality of doing so. All stakeholders are not equal, and pretending that they are does a disservice to those not protected in corporate law or left out of the process entirely.

Codes of conduct allow for greater participation as workers could potentially be involved with the drafting of codes of conduct. Having greater worker voice in the governance mechanisms may be a form of legitimacy, as those who are impacted by the code are instrumental in its drafting.[11] I use empirical research conducted by Professor Richard Locke as well as other scholars to provide evidence for the efficacy of codes.

My research is unique because there is not much research done at the intersection of corporate law and labour and employment law. It is often the case that labour law is studied at law schools and in political science, philosophy, and industrial relations departments. Corporate law is studied in law schools, business schools, and social science departments. The solution I offer of a code of conduct allows for greater worker voice in the governance of the workplace itself. The code is malleable so it can be changed to reflect changes in the workplace. I stress that beyond changing hard law and implementing soft law mechanisms like codes, there must be changes on the ground. I offer a pro-friendly approach that states that management should seek to create a more civil workplace for various reasons. But fundamentally, the research shows that a happy worker is a productive worker; so by being kind to workers, management

9 Peer Zumbansen & Simon Archer, "The BCE Decision: Reflections on the Firm as a Contractual Organization" (2008) Comparative Research in Law & Political Economy. Research Paper No 17/2008, online: <http://digitalcommons.osgoode.yorku.ca/clpe/191>, at 12.

10 Peer Zumbansen & Simon Archer, "The BCE Decision: Reflections on the Firm as a Contractual Organization" (2008) Comparative Research in Law & Political Economy. Research Paper No 17/2008, online: <http://digitalcommons.osgoode.yorku.ca/clpe/191>, at 9.

11 See the work in labour law about collective agreements and worker voice.

is able to gain productivity from the worker as well as decreased absence rates. This is operating out of enlightened self-interest in that what works for management is to be kind to workers in order to make more profit from workers.

Balancing the voice of the worker in the workplace setting has to be done with balancing the voice of the shareholder when the worker is employed at a corporation. Worker voice and shareholder voice rarely intersect in scholarship, but both have weight and importance.

Workers who try to gain success through legislative changes, such as the gains granted under the Wynne government in Ontario, can easily lose those gains when a new Premier is elected – Ford clawed back much of the change that the Wynne government put in place. These fleeting glimpses of gains for workers can easily be dismantled when a new government gets elected. Workers who rely on support for their children and have no health care at work also experience greater losses when the government plans to get rid of full-day kindergarten and eliminates the free coverage for prescriptions put in place for those under 25 years of age. So not only do workers lose in their workplace, but those who are lower middle class also lose important government support when a new government comes into power.

The fight to increase corporate transparency and accountability tends to be centred on reducing corporate crime such as insider trading rather than focused on increasing the rights of workers. So even when new caselaw is handed down from the SCC, it helps create greater progress but does not necessarily benefit workers. Advancements in CSR do not necessarily mean an increase in workers' rights, as those issues could focus on corporate crime and environmental protections rather than on workers. Overall the Canadian legal landscape has helped increase corporate accountability through *BCE* and *Chevron*, but neither of those cases helps workers.

The noted failures of Bill C-300 in Canada which focused on Corporate Accountability of Mining and the sections of Dodd-Frank in the United States of America that focused on conflict minerals being ruled unconstitutional demonstrate the difficulty in getting hard law passed that holds corporations accountable. Or, in the case of Dodd-Frank conflict minerals section, even if a law gets enacted, it can be repealed. This shows the limitations of hard law in a way that can be bypassed at the corporate level by the enactment of a code of conduct. This allows the corporation to be held accountable no matter in what jurisdiction the corporation operates. This again is another limitation of hard law as a nation state can only enact laws that pertain to its land in order to recognize and respect the sovereignty of other nation states. Because multinational corporations exist and operate in numerous jurisdictions, a mechanism needs to be in place that governs the corporate conduct beyond the territorial lines.

Along with the rise of CSR and the fact that it has become somewhat ingrained in the corporate culture of numerous corporations, there is also the work of international law scholars like John Ruggie to help with corporations accepting more responsibilities. The Ruggie Report outlines that nation states have a duty to *protect* human rights and that the corporation has a responsibility to *respect* human rights. The different burdens placed on nation states versus corporations is needed, but to consider that corporations did not fall under the purview of the UN until the 1990s seems to make clear that corporations have risen to a power that rivals nation states.[12] Canadian corporate law has changed, too. The *BCE* decision by the Supreme Court of Canada in 2008 has aligned Canadian corporate law away from the shareholder primacy model of the corporation towards stakeholder theory being actualized. In that decision the Court held that Directors must consider the interests of stakeholders beyond simply shareholders in the corporate decision-making process. This does not elevate stakeholders to the same level as shareholders but does increase the position of stakeholders from before. After *BCE* the decisions in *Choc v Hudbay*[13] and *Chevron*[14] outline that Canadian corporations have obligations even when operating on foreign soil. The Court is looking for ways to hold Canadian

12 See Adolf A. Berle & Gardiner C. Means, *The Modern Corporation and Private Property* (NJ: Transaction Publishers, 1991),.

13 *Choc v Hudbay Minerals Inc* 2013 ONSC 1414.
Hudbay Minerals is a Canadian mining company and the cause of action was that the corporation and its subsidiaries were committing human rights abuses by shooting, killing, and raping those who were against their mining project. Angelica Choc alleges that her husband, Adolfo Ich, was killed by the head of security at the Guatemalan Nickel Company. Justice Brown explores the notion of the corporation as a distinct legal entity and what grounds allow for the piercing of the corporate veil. It explores whether the corporation is able to sue and be sued regarding tort claims. The case rests on the position that the corporation can be sued for acts done by the security company it hired to guard a mine in Guatemala. The Mayans also assert that their human rights were abused by Hudbay. There were three actions, for ease of reference I will refer to them as: Angelica Choc claim, Margarita Caal Caal claim, and German Chub Choc claim. Amnesty International Canada was granted intervener status. Counsel for the defendants argued that there was no reasonable cause of action for the claims.

One of the main issues was about whether a parent company owes a supervisory duty to its subsidiaries. How much liability, if any, does Hudbay owe to HMI and CGN? The defendants argued that a parent company cannot be held liable for the actions of its subsidiaries. The defendants argued that allowing the suit to go forward would be to overturn the principles enunciated in *Salomon* more than one hundred years prior that the corporate entity is legally distinct. The court notes that most of the claims are based on direct corporate liability and only in the Angelica Choc claim does the plaintiff argue that the corporate veil should be pierced. The judge found that the *Anns* test for a novel duty of care was possibly met and there was no reason to not allow the claim to go forward on the argument that there was no reasonable cause of action. The judge struck all three motions. This case is decided in the light of *BCE* which allowed for greater accountability and transparency to be imposed on to corporations. *BCE* also increased the weight of transnational law on corporations.

14 *Chevron Corp v Yaiguaje* 2015 SCC 42.
In *Chevron* the case builds on the theories outlined in *BCE* and *Choc v Hudbay*. This is outlined in paragraph 95 of the decision which quotes from *BCE*. The court was tasked with deciding if an Ontario court has jurisdiction to enforce a court order from Ecuador. The test is whether there is a real and substantial connection. "Jurisdiction also exists here with respect to Chevron Canada because it was validly served at a place of business it operates in the province." The court did not accept the argument that this

corporations liable for atrocities committed on foreign soil back to Canadian courtrooms. Again, this links back to John Ruggie's work about nation states versus corporations, but also to the notion that victims should have greater access to justice. It seems that the Court has made a decision that Canada will be a beacon for human rights and will stretch Canadian law to accommodate victims of corporate abuses if the abuse is done by a Canadian corporation. This widens the reach of Canadian law, but in an era of CSR and increased corporate accountability, this seems rather in step, not out of place with the rest of the world.

Definition of terms

The term "corporate social responsibility" is used to differentiate from the former model of corporations existing merely for their shareholders and to increase profit and means that corporations have duties to other stakeholders beyond shareholders.[15] Those stakeholders include, but are not limited to, employees, the environment, and government. The definition of CSR itself is debated among academics and practitioners. In his 1999 article Archie Carroll outlines the history of the definition of CSR.[16] One of the most important definitions is the one devised by Keith Davis:

> For the purposes of this discussion it [CSR] refers to the firm's consideration of, and response to, issues beyond the narrow economic, technical, and legal requirements of the firm.[17]

Another definition explored by Carroll is the one provided by S. Prakash Sethi: "social obligation in corporate behaviour 'in response to market forces or legal constraints.'"[18] The definition that will be used for this book is the one developed by the Corporate Social Responsibility Initiative at the Harvard Kennedy School of Government:

> Corporate social responsibility encompasses not only what companies do with their profits, but also how they make them. It goes beyond philanthropy and compliance and addresses how companies manage their economic, social, and environmental impacts, as well as their relationships in

would be a piercing of the corporate veil. Nor was it against the ruling in *BCE* about corporate separateness.

15 See Freeman and stakeholder theory.

16 Archie Carroll, "Corporate Social Responsibility: Evolution of a Definitional Construct" *Business & Society* vol 38 no 3 (Sep. 1999) pp. 268–295.

17 Archie Carroll, "Corporate Social Responsibility: Evolution of a Definitional Construct" *Business & Society* vol 38 no 3 (Sep. 1999) pp. 268–295 at 277.

18 Archie Carroll, "Corporate Social Responsibility: Evolution of a Definitional Construct" *Business & Society* vol 38 no 3 (Sep. 1999) pp. 268–295 at 279.

> all key spheres of influence: the workplace, the marketplace, the supply chain, the community, and the public policy realm.[19]

I chose this definition because of its focus on the workplace as the first item listed. The workplace is the central focus of this book, which examines how corporations can be instrumental in increasing the rights of workers. Workplaces can be governed by both CSR concepts and soft law mechanisms.

"Soft law" can be defined as the use of codes of conduct, governmental norms, voluntary standards, the work of advocacy groups, and other stakeholders in shaping the responsibilities of corporations. The term "hard law" is used to refer to legislation and legally binding agreements. "Soft law, so defined, comes in many forms, from private and voluntary codes and certification and labelling systems to transparency obligations on the part of governments."[20] Hard law and soft law can also be thought of as a continuum. Also, within both terms there exist further spectrums.

> In both theory and, over time, in practice, both hard law and soft law have distinct, if not always unique, advantages and disadvantages of their own. Hard law offers the legitimacy, the strong surveillance and enforcement mechanisms, and the guaranteed resources that soft law often lacks.[21]

Definitions of the term "workers' rights" are as varied as the definitions of CSR. Workers' rights can be as basic as fighting for essential rights like the fight for a living wage to more "advanced" rights such as the right to strike and the right to bargain collectively. For the purpose of this book, the term "workers' rights" includes remuneration, wages and benefits, working hours, overtime compensation, no child labour, no forced labour, health and safety, non-discrimination, and harassment or abuse.

Background

This introductory chapter reviews the literature on CSR theory and the literature on workers' rights. While this book is at the intersection of the two subjects, it is worth noting that the literature on the two areas rarely intersects.

19 Harvard Kennedy School of Government, online: <www.hks.harvard.edu/m-rcbg/CSRI/init_approach.html>.

20 John Kirton & Michael Trebilcock, eds., *Hard Choices, Soft Law: Voluntary Standards in Global Trade, Environment and Social Governance* (Cornwall: Ashgate Publishing Limited, 2004), at 10.

21 Janis Sarra, "The Corporation as Symphony: Are Shareholders First Violin or Second Fiddle?" *University of British Columbia Law Review* vol 36 (2003) pp. 403–442 at 11.

Corporate social responsibility

The CSR literature encompasses a broad spectrum from those authors who believe that true change can be achieved through the work of corporations modifying the nature of their business, implementing codes of conduct, etc., to those authors who are sceptical of the entire CSR movement.

The debate about CSR can be traced to the essential text in the study of CSR within law, which is Berle and Means's work *The Modern Corporation and Private Property*.[22] This book lays the foundation for the discussion of CSR and the real role that corporations play in society. In *The Modern Corporation and Private Property*, the authors outline their theory about the role of the corporation in society.

> The most enduring theme of *The Modern Corporation and Private Property* is the divorce of ownership from the control of the modern corporation. . . . [A]s a practical matter, stockholders have traded their legal position of private ownership for the role of recipient of capital returns (Book I, Chapter I). In addition, a close parallel is drawn between workers who surrender the direction over their labor and shareholders who become merely recipients of "the wages of capital."[23]

Fundamental works such as that done by Berle and Means and the work of Milton Friedman have shaped the CSR theories and discourse. In the article "The Social Responsibility of Business is to Increase Profits,"[24] Friedman states that businessmen who speak about business' social conscience are: "[i]n fact they are – or would be if they or anyone took them seriously preaching pure and unadulterated socialism. Businessmen who talk this way are unwittingly puppets of the intellectual forces that have been undermining the basis of a free society these past decades."[25] It is worth noting that Friedman raises the issue of socialism, as he was writing in a time of the "red scare" where countries, America in particular, feared the spread of Communism to their nations.

> The discussions of the "social responsibilities of business" are notable for their analytical looseness and lack of rigor. What does it mean to say that "business" has responsibilities? Only people can have responsibilities. A corporation is an artificial person and in this sense may have artificial

22 Adolf Berle & Gardiner Means, *The Modern Corporation and Private Property* (New York: The MacMillan Company, 1932).
23 Adolf A. Berle & Gardiner C. Means, *The Modern Corporation and Private Property* (New Brunswick, NJ: Transaction Publishers, 1991), at ix.
24 Milton Friedman, "The Social Responsibility of Business Is to Increase Its Profits" *The New York Times Magazine*, Sep. 13 1970.
25 Milton Friedman, "The Social Responsibility of Business Is to Increase Its Profits" *The New York Times Magazine*, Sep. 13 1970 at 1.

> responsibilities, but "business" as a whole cannot be said to have responsibilities, even in this vague sense. The first step toward clarity in examining the doctrine of the social responsibility of business is to ask precisely what it implies for whom.[26]

However, there is the notion that corporations can "do good by being good" which is in regard to corporations that brand themselves as socially responsible and may actually increase their consumer base and profits as a result. This is termed the "business case"[27] for CSR by business management scholars. Friedman states that, "there is one and only one social responsibility of business – to use its resources and engage in activities designed to increase its profits so long as it stays within the rules of the game, which is to say, engages in open and free competition without deception or fraud."[28] However, the challenge to Friedman is, what happens when the rules of the game change? Refraining from deception and fraud is not sufficient.

Berle and Means discuss the division between ownership and control, which is very important in that those who are now in control, management, have to create their role in terms of their relation to the owners, the shareholders. "Though the law still maintains the conception of a sharp dividing line recognizing the bondholder as a lender of capital and the stockholder as a quasi-partner in the enterprise, economically the positions of the two have drawn together."[29] This distinction between investors such as shareholders, who are held to be the owners of the corporation, and bondholders, who may be limited to the terms of their contract, is important and nuanced. While the shareholders are the legal owners of the corporation, the role of the bondholders as another subset of investors needs to be detailed.

> In the present study we have treated the stockholders of a corporation as its owners. When speaking of the ownership of all corporations, the bondholders are often included with the stockholders as part owners. The economist does not hesitate for certain purposes to class an employee with wages due him as temporarily a part owner. All of these groups have interests in the enterprise. Yet a laborer who has a very real interest in the business in so far as it can continue to give him employment is not regarded as part owner.[30]

26 Milton Friedman, "The Social Responsibility of Business Is to Increase Its Profits" *The New York Times Magazine*, Sep. 13 1970 at 1.
27 Professor Dirk Matten's work among others.
28 Milton Friedman, "The Social Responsibility of Business Is to Increase Its Profits" *The New York Times Magazine*, Sep. 13 1970 at 6.
29 Adolf A. Berle & Gardiner C. Means, *The Modern Corporation and Private Property* (New Brunswick, NJ: Transaction Publishers, 1991), at 246.
30 Adolf A. Berle & Gardiner C. Means, *The Modern Corporation and Private Property* (New Brunswick, NJ: Transaction Publishers, 1991), at 113.

The authors also examine the role of the state in regards to how a corporation functions in a capitalist society.

> Corporations derive their profits partly indeed from their own operations, but partly also from their market position and increasingly from techniques resulting from state expenditures of taxpayers' money. In this sense, the American state is an investor in practically every substantial enterprise; without its activity, the enterprise, if it could exist at all, would be or would have been compelled to spend money and effort to create position, maintain access to market, and build technical development it currently takes for granted.[31]

The state acquiesces to give up some of its power to the corporation. Berle and Means comment on how the state is an accomplice in its own demise in the corporate revolution.

Berle and Means note that the power of the shareholder lessens as the number of shareholders increases. And they posit that perhaps shareholders do not deserve the spoils given to them. "Stockholders toil not, neither do they spin, to earn that reward."[32] The role of the Industrial Revolution as described by Berle and Means gives much weight to an alternate view than purely capitalistic.

> Like the industrial revolution, which established the factory as a predominant form of production and separated the worker from control over the instruments of production, the corporate revolution, separating ownership from control over the instruments of production, has come on us gradually.[33]

Berle and Means go on to state that "Profits are an essential part of the corporate system. But the use of corporate power solely to serve the stockholders is no longer likely to serve the public interest."[34] The movement from the shareholder primacy theory leading to benefits for society as a whole was being reformed as the theory that everyone benefits leads to the stakeholder model. Rather than making everyone in society inadvertent beneficiaries, as in shareholder primacy, stakeholder theory makes stakeholders direct beneficiaries.

31 Adolf A. Berle & Gardiner C. Means, *The Modern Corporation and Private Property* (New Brunswick, NJ: Transaction Publishers, 1991), at xxviii.
32 Adolf A. Berle & Gardiner C. Means, *The Modern Corporation and Private Property* (New Brunswick, NJ: Transaction Publishers, 1991), at xxxv.
33 Adolf A. Berle & Gardiner C. Means, *The Modern Corporation and Private Property* (New Brunswick, NJ: Transaction Publishers, 1991), at xlii.
34 Adolf A. Berle & Gardiner C. Means, *The Modern Corporation and Private Property* (New Brunswick, NJ: Transaction Publishers, 1991), at xlvii.

Berle and Means also note that the separation of ownership and control has created more than merely a passive property owner, but one that may be rather more disinterested than an actual owner.

> Finally, in the corporate system, the "owner" of industrial wealth is left with a mere symbol of ownership while the power, the responsibility and the substance which have been an integral part of ownership in the past are being transferred to a separate group in whose hands lies control.[35]

Also, the transient nature of owning shares as opposed to a permanent owner is another consideration. "In discussing problems of enterprise it is possible to distinguish between three functions: that of having interests in an enterprise, that of having power over it, and that of acting with respect to it."[36] Shareholders can be described as holding passive property in a way that differs from owning a house or a car.

> Over a decade ago, Walter Rathenau wrote concerning the German counterpart of our great corporation: "No one is a permanent owner. The composition of the thousandfold complex which functions as lord of the undertaking is in a state depersonalized . . . The depersonalization of ownership simultaneously implies the objectification of the thing owned."[37]

Workers' rights are not often discussed in the context of corporate law, but Berle and Means argued that this should not be the case because of the importance to corporations of a well-trained and hardworking workforce for a corporation.

> It is conceivable, – indeed it seems almost essential if the corporate system is to survive, – that the 'control' of the great corporations should develop into a purely neutral technocracy, balancing a variety of claims by various groups in the community and assigning to each a portion of the income stream on the basis of public policy rather than private cupidity.[38]

The last page of the book leaves the reader with the notion that transnational corporations may have more power than the nation state:

35 Adolf A. Berle & Gardiner C. Means, *The Modern Corporation and Private Property* (New Brunswick, NJ: Transaction Publishers, 1991), at 65.
36 Adolf A. Berle & Gardiner C. Means, *The Modern Corporation and Private Property* (New Brunswick, NJ: Transaction Publishers, 1991), at 112.
37 Adolf A. Berle & Gardiner C. Means, *The Modern Corporation and Private Property* (New Brunswick, NJ: Transaction Publishers, 1991), at 309.
38 Adolf A. Berle & Gardiner C. Means, *The Modern Corporation and Private Property* (New Brunswick, NJ: Transaction Publishers, 1991), at 312–313.

> The rise of the modern corporation has brought a concentration of economic power which can compete on equal terms with the modern state – economic power versus political power, each strong in its own field. The state seeks in some aspects to regulate the corporation, while the corporation, steadily becoming more powerful, makes every effort to avoid such regulation. Where its own interests are concerned, it even attempts to dominate the state. The future may see the economic organism, now typified by the corporation, not only on an equal plane with the state, but possibly even superseding it as the dominant form of social organization.[39]

This discussion about the nation state being surpassed by the corporation as the governing entity is still relevant today as the governance gap shows.

Professor Jagdish Bhagwati, an Economics Professor at Columbia University, builds on Berle and Means's notion that the corporation may rival the nation state for power. "Of course, there is a further argument that the entire democratic process is illegitimate because corporations have captured it, that freer trade and direct investment lobbies are pushing for such integration of the world economy."[40] The corporate revolution, as Berle and Means has termed it, has created an entity that may be able to escape the control of national governments and then on to the world. Bhagwati notes that lower working standards may not necessarily lead to abuse, as multinational corporations may not make use of these lower standards.

> [J]ust because lower standards exist in the poor countries, it does not follow that multinationals will take advantage of them. The gains to be made by doing so can be outweighed by several economic factors. Take just reputational effects. The multinationals, which account for an overwhelming percentage of direct foreign investment in the poor countries, cannot afford to be seen to dump dangerous effluents into the waters or into the air or treat their workers badly.[41]

The question then becomes: why would multinationals not use these lowered standards to their advantage? Is there some moral mechanism in place that prevents them from doing so? Even if corporations do not make use of these lax standards, one can still make the argument that even if the corporations did make use of them, the corporation's reputation may not suffer as a result.

Sometimes the efforts by advocacy groups and NGOs are seen to be paternalistic in that rich nations tell poor nations what is good for them. "It is not

39 Adolf A. Berle & Gardiner C. Means, *The Modern Corporation and Private Property* (New Brunswick, NJ: Transaction Publishers, 1991), at 313.

40 Jagdish Bhagwati, *In Defense of Globalization* (New York: Oxford University Press, 2007), at 103.

41 Jagdish Bhagwati, *In Defense of Globalization* (New York: Oxford University Press, 2007), at 130.

surprising, therefore, that this political posturing by our labor and environmental groups is occasionally seen in poor countries, including by some unions and environmental NGOs there, as a kind of neo-imperialism."[42] Bhagwati's claim that these efforts may be seen to be neo-imperialism is valid as this argument gets raised by many. However, the alternative may be to remain silent and allow abuses to continue because those in poor nations are perhaps not able to fight or are in fact unaware of the abuse in the first place.

The literature seems to be divided between those who think that CSR is effective and can help to increase the rights of workers, and those who are sceptical. Certain authors spend vast amounts of time shaping and molding the definition of CSR, and the debate and determinations flow from that definition.[43] Other authors[44] such as Sisodia, Wolfe, and Sheth, argue that it is in the best interests of corporations to brand themselves as socially responsible. Those corporations are also better able to endear themselves to existing and potential customers. It seems to create or increase brand loyalty among existing customers and to increase the corporations' consumer base by attracting new "ethical consumers." "The search for meaning is changing expectations in that marketplace, and in the workplace. Indeed, we believe it is changing the very soul of capitalism."[45] Their arguments differ slightly from the typical arguments in favour of CSR in that the authors state that corporations that are almost more lovable are better able to prosper. This may include such corporations as the Body Shop and American Apparel, which seem to attract customers to buy their products and let them leave those stores with a sense of activism in that the products they have just purchased are "doing good for the world."[46]

Certain aspects of CSR have become so ingrained that we may forget the origin. From the rise of the electric car and non-GMO products to FairTrade consumers have been a driving force behind corporate changes.[47]

Wayne Visser and others[48] raise many interesting questions about corporations: "In whose interest do they act? To whom are they accountable? What practices

42 Jagdish Bhagwati, *In Defense of Globalization* (New York: Oxford University Press, 2007), at 132.

43 Geoffrey Heal, *When Principles Pay: Corporate Social Responsibility and the Bottom Line* (New York: Columbia University Press, 2008), at 2.

44 Sisodia Rajendra, David B. Wolfe & Jagdish N. Sheth, Firms of Endearment: How World-Class Companies Profit from Passion and Purpose (Philadelphia: Wharton School Publishing, 2007).

45 Sisodia Rajendra, David B. Wolfe & Jagdish N. Sheth, Firms of Endearment: How World-Class Companies Profit from Passion and Purpose (Philadelphia: Wharton School Publishing, 2007), at 4.

46 See also Toms, the shoe company. For every pair of shoes purchased, the company states that they will donate a pair of shoes to a child in Africa.

47 Andrew Crane et al., *The Oxford Handbook of Corporate Social Responsibility* (Oxford: Oxford University Press, 2008), at 288.

48 Wayne Visser et al., *The A to Z of Corporate Social Responsibility: A Complete Guide to Concepts, Codes and Organisations* (West Sussex: John Wiley & Sons Ltd, 2007).

are they using?"[49] The authors discuss ethical consumerism. "Ethical consumption refers to retail customers' opting for goods that are perceived to create more preferable social economic or environmental impacts and outcomes than competing equivalent."[50]

The work of Lawrence Mitchell[51] is useful because it discusses how corporations in North America often commit their abuses in other countries. His work highlights how to combat abuses internationally. This also raises the issue of risk management and how corporations should end their international abuses because it opens them up to liability and risk.

> American corporate law ignores workers. They don't figure into the structure of the corporation or its legal duties. But there is no one group of people more identified with a corporation and more responsible for its day-to-day conduct than corporate workers.[52]

Geoffrey Heal's[53] work argues that corporations that adhere to CSR are better able to sell their products. Essentially, corporations that brand themselves as socially responsible are able to tap into the ethical consumer base.

> It is a system in which the forces that I describe . . . have grown stronger and become more clearly articulated – a system where consumers and civil society groups, together with activist shareholders and SRI funds, play an increasing role in shaping the incentives faced by the corporate world. It is a system in which principles pay.[54]

Heal notes that

> I am instead going to investigate the forces that drive their behavior in these areas and argue that, perhaps surprisingly to some, there are growing

49 Wayne Visser et al., *The A to Z of Corporate Social Responsibility: A Complete Guide to Concepts, Codes and Organisations* (West Sussex: John Wiley & Sons Ltd, 2007), at Introduction x.

50 Wayne Visser et al., *The A to Z of Corporate Social Responsibility: A Complete Guide to Concepts, Codes and Organisations* (West Sussex: John Wiley & Sons Ltd, 2007), at 195.

51 Lawrence E. Mitchell, *Corporate Irresponsibility: America's Newest Export* (New Haven: Yale University Press, 2001).

52 Lawrence E. Mitchell, *Corporate Irresponsibility: America's Newest Export* (New Haven: Yale University Press, 2001), at 208.

53 Geoffrey Heal, *When Principles Pay: Corporate Social Responsibility and the Bottom Line* (New York: Columbia University Press, 2008).

54 Geoffrey Heal, *When Principles Pay: Corporate Social Responsibility and the Bottom Line* (New York: Columbia University Press, 2008), at Preface xiii.

> forces that make it in a company's financial interest to be concerned about its social and environmental footprint.[55]

The issues of equity and fairness are worth exploring:

> This is a debate about the acceptability of market outcomes in terms of fairness and equity. Is it reasonable that the people who make our shoes or clothes should work ten hours or more daily for one or two dollars? Is it reasonable that children should work in these conditions? If not, whom should we charge with responsibility for remedying this situation and how should they go about it?[56]

How external members of society view a company is an issue that arises in the CSR literature. Heal argues that the triple bottom line is more relevant than previously thought. "So it can be in a company's interest to pay more than is strictly necessary to retain its labor force, contributing both to its bottom line and to developing a reputation for being a good employer and being socially responsible."[57] When compiling evidence to determine the best way to measure CSR, it is worth noting that profit may be a poor choice. The reason that profit is a bad indicator of CSR is that "[s]ome industries just have higher rates of profit than others."[58]

Moses L. Pava and Joshua Krausz[59] note that

> [s]ocial responsibility does not cause enhanced financial performance; rather, financial performance allows for the performance of discretionary social actions. Much anecdotal evidence supports this view. Our conclusion, however, is that it may not be accurate to suggest that the demands for social responsibility are always external to the corporation, as the stakeholder model (as developed by Ullmann) implies.[60]

Simon Zadek's[61] work is useful because it examines the CSR debate outside of simply a legal framework. The author does a great job of summarizing key points in the CSR literature. "Nobel Prize-winning economist Milton Friedman

55 Geoffrey Heal, *When Principles Pay: Corporate Social Responsibility and the Bottom Line* (New York: Columbia University Press, 2008), at 2.

56 Geoffrey Heal, *When Principles Pay: Corporate Social Responsibility and the Bottom Line* (New York: Columbia University Press, 2008), at 14.

57 Geoffrey Heal, *When Principles Pay: Corporate Social Responsibility and the Bottom Line* (New York: Columbia University Press, 2008), at 27.

58 Geoffrey Heal, *When Principles Pay: Corporate Social Responsibility and the Bottom Line* (New York: Columbia University Press, 2008), at 29.

59 Moses L. Pava & Joshua Krausz, *Corporate Responsibility and Financial Performance: The Paradox of Social Cost* (Westport: Quorum Books, 1995).

60 Moses L. Pava & Joshua Krausz, *Corporate Responsibility and Financial Performance: The Paradox of Social Cost* (Westport: Quorum Books, 1995), at 150.

61 Simon Zadek, *The Civil Corporation* (London: Earthscan, 2007).

Table 1.1 Seven principles

Principle 1	Integrated, Sustainable Decision-making: Corporate decision-makers must consider environmental and social issues, in addition to economic considerations, when carrying out their duties and responsibilities
Principle 2	Stakeholder Engagement: Corporations must engage not only with shareholders, but also with stakeholders generally, on environmental and social issues within the corporate sphere of influence
Principle 3	Transparency: Corporations must provide periodic public reports on their environmental and social performance and disclose material information relating to environmental and social matters within their sphere of influence
Principle 4	Consistent Best Practices: Whether at home or abroad, corporations must seek to apply the highest environmental and social standards throughout their operations and during their interactions with their business partners
Principle 5	Precautionary Principle: An absence of conclusive scientific evidence that serious and irreversible environmental harm will occur within their sphere of influence must not deter corporations from taking cost-effective precautionary measures. Furthermore, corporations bear the burden of proof of socially acceptable safety when they advocate potentially harmful projects
Principle 6	Accountability: Corporations and their decision-makers must be held accountable both for environmental and social harms and for failure to meet their own proclaimed standards of ethical conduct
Principle 7	Community Investment: Corporations must undertake programs and initiatives that contribute to the social, cultural, economic, or environmental enrichment of the communities in which they operate

Source: Michael Kerr, Richard Janda, & Chip Pitts, *Corporate Social Responsibility: A Legal Analysis* (Toronto: LexisNexis Canada Inc., 2009), at 91.

felt at ease encouraging businesses to 'be responsible' by making as much money as possible because he envisaged economies disciplined by governments that were more or less accountable to the people."[62] The author offers answers to why things don't change – "inertia, inaction."[63]

Michael Kerr, Richard Janda, and Chip Pitts[64] lay out core principles that corporations should implement to be able to actually brand themselves as socially responsible. This is demonstrated by seven principles.

The existing literature on CSR has many gaps, such as the link between positive actions and responsibilities on the part of corporations and the benefit experienced, if any, by workers. While having corporations be more responsible in broad terms

62 Simon Zadek, *The Civil Corporation* (London: Earthscan, 2007), at 1.

63 Simon Zadek, *The Civil Corporation* (London: Earthscan, 2007), at 46.

64 Michael Kerr, Richard Janda, & Chip Pitts, *Corporate Social Responsibility: A Legal Analysis* (Toronto: LexisNexis Canada Inc., 2009).

is unlikely to be objectionable, the benefit bestowed on workers may be minimal, if there is any at all. The strands that I will pick up and expand upon in my research includes the correlation between CSR and the rights of workers in that an increase in social responsibility on the part of corporations may not directly impact the rights of workers but instead may include or mean things such as an increase in charitable donations or increased environmental protections. While both may help workers indirectly, the nature of direct links must be explored.

Shareholder primacy model

Milton Friedman and other scholars advocate for a shareholder primacy model of the corporation, one in which shareholders are the primary concern of the corporation in the form of wealth-maximization for shareholders. It is commonly held that shareholders are the true owners of the corporation because their investment is what allows for the corporation to function. They also have powers to remove and elect a new Board of Directors. Shareholders are also residual claimants as they would be the ones who gain any excess on sale of the company or, in case of bankruptcy, would lose all of their investment. While bondholders (also termed "debentureholders") are investors, too, their investment is contract-driven and not the same as shareholders who open themselves up to risk by investing in the corporation. Because of the nature of the relationship that shareholders have with the corporation it is held that Directors have a fiduciary duty to shareholders. In Canada, Section 122 of the CBCA outlines Directors' Duties. Common law duties also exist. Section 122 states:

122. 1 Every director and officer of a corporation in exercising their powers and discharging their duties shall

a act honestly and in good faith with a view to the best interests of the corporation; and

b exercise the care, diligence and skill that a reasonably prudent person would exercise in comparable circumstances.

Duty to comply

2 Every director and officer of a corporation shall comply with this Act, the regulations, articles, by-laws and any unanimous shareholder agreement.

No exculpation

3 Subject to subsection 146(5), no provision in a contract, the articles, the by-laws or a resolution relieves a director or officer from the duty to act in accordance with this Act or the regulations or relieves them from liability for a breach thereof.[65]

65 *Canada Business Corporations Act*, R.S.C. 1985, c. C-44, s. 122.

While Directors have statutory obligations as outlined in Section 122 of the *CBCA*, there are also duties at common law that make an impact on assessing whether or not a Director has fulfilled their obligations to the corporation. Fiduciary duties entail the utmost fidelity and loyalty. Shareholder primacy was the governing theory which held that shareholders were the primary concern for Directors. This could be extended to Directors of a corporation owing a fiduciary duty to shareholders and shareholders alone. Modern stakeholder theory holds that Directors have duties to other stakeholders beyond merely shareholders, such as employees, customers, suppliers, communities, and even the environment. With the *Peoples*[66] and *BCE*[67] decisions being handed down in Canada, the nature of Directors' duties has to be re-assessed.[68] The discussion of shareholder primacy leads to the discussion of stakeholder theory and how other stakeholders beyond shareholders need to be considered when Directors make decisions.

The corporation and the corporate form is not fixed. It is malleable and can be amended. Writing in 1932, Dodd states that "[t]he business is still a private enterprise existing for the profit of its owners, who are now the stockholders . . . The directors and other agents are fiduciaries carrying on the business in the sole interest of the stockholders."[69] Shareholder primacy still holds up this version, but even Dodd states that there are leaders and laggards regarding leadership. "The principal object of legal compulsion might then be to keep those who failed to catch the new spirit up to the standards which their more enlightened competitors would desire to adopt voluntarily."[70] This seems akin to CSR theory which posits that there are leaders and laggards in regards to CSR corporate leaders which draw in the laggards to compete with more socially responsible companies. "Nevertheless there are indications that even today corporation managers not infrequently use corporate funds in ways which suggest a social responsibility rather than exclusively profit-making viewpoint."[71] Dodd goes on to discuss corporate philanthropy, which is still debateable whether that is in fact CSR, but it does run against agency theory in the construct that the corporation is to serve the best interests of the shareholders. Unless the business case for CSR is used, this may lead to the thinking that making corporate donations may increase profit in the long term.

The business case for CSR is put forward as a way for businesses to gain while saving the planet. One example is saving energy costs which helps the

66 *Peoples Department Stores v. Wise*, 2004 SCC 68.
67 *BCE Inc. v.* 1976 *Debentureholders*, 2008 SCC 69.
68 There will be a further discussion on *Peoples* and *BCE* later on.
69 E. Merrick Dodd, "For Whom Are Corporate Managers Trustees?" *Harvard Law Review* vol 45 no 7 (May 1932) pp. 1145–1163 at 1146.
70 E. Merrick Dodd, "For Whom Are Corporate Managers Trustees?" *Harvard Law Review* vol 45 no 7 (May 1932) pp. 1145–1163 at 1153.
71 E. Merrick Dodd, "For Whom Are Corporate Managers Trustees?" *Harvard Law Review* vol 45 no 7 (May 1932) pp. 1145–1163 at 1158.

environment and helps the company save money. This raises a similar issue as the one in Benefit Corporations, as those Directors are meant to serve other interests beyond shareholders as exemplified by the specific purpose of the Benefit Corporation and the general purpose as well.

> Management may never have promised customers, employees, suppliers, etc. a "return on investment," but management is nevertheless obliged to take seriously its extra-legal obligations not to injure, lie to or cheat these stakeholders *quite apart from* whether it is in the stockholders' interests.[72]

David Vogel

David Vogel's work on governance is important because he notes that private governance or non-state governance is not a new phenomenon outside of business. "'Governance without government' has long been observed and theorized by political scientists (e.g. Rosenau and Czempiel 1992)."[73] Vogel goes on to state that codes of conduct that deal with labour-related issues are not well-studied beyond case studies. "Although there have been several studies of the impact of labor codes, they are primarily based on case studies, which are not necessarily representative. There are few scholarly studies of the effectiveness of most civil regulations."[74]

Peter Utting

Peter Utting notes that consumer activism "involves efforts to inform consumers about specific products or companies, organise consumer boycotts, and ensure that companies and consumers in the North pay a fair price to small producers in the South."[75] This relates to ethical consumption and the notion that some consumers make their purchasing choices based on ethical standards. "Rather than seeing corporate self-regulation and voluntary approaches as a superior alternative to governmental and international regulation, the corporate accountability agenda suggests a re-articulation of voluntary and legal approaches."[76] This statement is essential because CSR is about voluntary mechanisms, and my book looks at how this relates to the legal mechanisms in place.

72 Kenneth E. Goodpaster, "Business Ethics and Stakeholder Analysis" *Business Ethics Quarterly* vol 1 no 1 (Jan. 1991) pp. 53–73 at 69–70 (emphasis in original).

73 David Vogel, "Private Global Business Regulation" *Annual Review of Political Science* vol 11 (2008) pp. 261–282 at 263.

74 David Vogel, "Private Global Business Regulation" *Annual Review of Political Science* vol 11 (2008) pp. 261–282 at 275.

75 Peter Utting, "Corporate Responsibility and the Movement of Business" *Development in Practice* vol 15 no 3/4 (June 2005) pp. 375–388 at 377.

76 Peter Utting, "Corporate Responsibility and the Movement of Business" *Development in Practice* vol 15 no 3/4 (June 2005) pp. 375–388 at 386.

Stakeholder theory

Berle's 1931 article brought to the forefront the need to consider who the corporation was really serving, be it shareholders, consumers, workers, etc. "In 1931, Berle advanced the notion that corporate directors would become subject to the implied oversight of a court's equitable jurisdiction and that, in the future, corporate law would become 'in substance, a branch of the law of trust.'"[77] As mentioned earlier in the discussion of Berle and Means, the notion that the shareholder is merely a passive owner is important. Why should the corporation serve the interests of a passive party that may be rather disinterested, when it can serve in the interests of those who are closer, arguably the consumers and employees?

> Now I submit that you can not abandon emphasis on "the view that business corporations exist for the sole purpose of making profits for their stockholders" until such time as you are prepared to offer a clear and reasonably enforceable scheme of responsibilities to someone else.[78]

Berle leaves the reader with the thought that the corporation should serve interests beyond merely those of shareholders and should serve broad interests. Is this truly the beginning of stakeholder theory? Possibly the beginning of CSR?

> Most students of corporation finance dream of a time when corporate administration will be held to a high degree of required responsibility – a responsibility conceived not merely in terms of stockholders' rights, but in terms of economic government satisfying the respective needs of investors, workers, customers, and the aggregated community.[79]

The typical rejoinder to a multi-stakeholder model is to argue that a duty to everyone is a duty to no one. "Serving two principals is a breach of fiduciary duty because it creates a de facto inability to serve with utmost good faith and fidelity."[80] Balancing competing interests may be achieved in the non fiduciary realm, but when discussing dual fiduciary duties, an apparent paradox arises. How is a Director to decide which stakeholders' interest will trump other stakeholders? Do profits win over the environment? Do profits win over workers?

77 Ed Waitzer & Johnny Jaswal, "Peoples, BCE, and the Good Corporate 'Citizen'" *Osgoode Hall Law Journal* (2009) pp. 439–496 at para 68.

78 Adolf A. Berle, "For Whom Corporate Managers Are Trustees: A Note" *Harvard Law Review* vol 45 no 8 (June 1932) pp. 1365–1372 at 1367.

79 Adolf A. Berle, "For Whom Corporate Managers Are Trustees: A Note" *Harvard Law Review* vol 45 no 8 (June 1932) pp. 1365–1372 at 1372.

80 Mark Ellis, *Fiduciary Duties in Canada, Looseleaf* (Toronto: Carswell, 2011), at para. 3–17.

This artificial balancing will lead to problems. It is trite to say that legislation on the books needs to be tested in the courts, but it is true that caselaw will help to interpret and understand the true limits of fiduciary duties in corporations' legislation. "It is poignantly clear that a duty premised upon fidelity, serving two or more parties may be a breach of duty."[81] How is a Director able to balance what seems to be dual fiduciary duties? It seems to be a paradox to ask someone to serve with the utmost fidelity while balancing seemingly contradicting interests. Hopefully, future caselaw will help to set parameters on the duties of Directors of Corporations and will make *BCE*, a stakeholder articulation by the Supreme Court of Canada, clear.

One of the leading authors in the area of stakeholder theory is R. Edward Freeman, as his work in the early 1980s was essential. "As outlined originally in Freeman (1984), stakeholder theory was concerned with the problem of value creation and trade."[82] This view is contrasted with the shareholder primacy model as outlined in Berle and Means.

> The stakeholder theory literature seems to represent an abrupt departure from the usual understanding of business as a vehicle to maximize returns to the owners of capital. This more mainstream view – call it "shareholder capitalism," or "the standard account" – has recently come under much criticism, and the "stakeholder view" is often put forward as an alternative.[83]

Stakeholder theory is linked with CSR. To bring progress the model should be changed to become more stakeholder-centric. Rather than the two models being separate and distinct, it may be that a new model which is in fact a merger of the two models may emerge. It is very much a symbiotic relationship between stakeholders and the corporation itself, as the two have a relationship that is important to each for different reasons.

> "Stakeholder capitalism" takes a different view – a company's overriding responsibility is to its stakeholders – because the corporation is both an economic and social institution. "It is not only the shareholders (who are here today, gone tomorrow) who have a legitimate stake in the enterprise, but also the employees, communities, and society as a whole" (Kuttner 1997: 190).[84]

81 Mark Ellis, *Fiduciary Duties in Canada, Looseleaf* (Toronto: Carswell, 2011), at para. 1-8.01.

82 R. Edward Freeman et al., *Stakeholder Theory: The State of the Art* (Cambridge: Cambridge University Press, 2010), at 4.

83 R. Edward Freeman et al., *Stakeholder Theory: The State of the Art* (Cambridge: Cambridge University Press, 2010), at xv.

84 Neil Gunningham & Joseph Rees, "Industry Self-Regulation: An Institutional Perspective" *Law and Policy* vol 19 no 4 (Oct. 1997) pp. 363–414 at 375.

Also, it is important to note that stakeholders are not a homogeneous group, nor is each stakeholder group homogeneous – not all employees have the same interests and concerns, nor do all consumers have the same interests and concerns, and so on.

> As Frederick (1978, 1994) defined it, corporate social responsiveness (or "CSR_2," to differentiate it from CSR_1 _ corporate social responsibility) is "the capacity of a corporation to respond to social pressures. The key questions are: Can the company respond? Will it? Does it? How does it? To what extent? And with that effect?" (Frederick 1994: 154).[85]

This is an important concern in that corporations may actually be restrained in how it may respond to certain issues. It is important for stakeholders to understand that the corporation may not be able to respond to all concerns and issues. CSR not only helps shareholders or other stakeholder groups but helps the corporation itself as a way to self-regulate and ensure that the corporation is being run smoothly and effectively.

> In this perspective, CSR, corporate governance, and stakeholder theory seem to converge: the firm is defined as a multi-stakeholder organization, where the individual groups collaborate (as in Evan and Freeman 1993) as long as they can rely on a fair exercise of the discretionary power by the management or, in other words, as long as the corporate governance mechanisms are fair.[86]

The notion of fairness is significant, as responsibility and duties are not the same as being fair. Fairness and justice are often intertwined as these both play an integral part of the justice system more broadly, and a democratic society should foster such key terms.

The role of government needs to be explored in relation to stakeholder theory. The state-centred model of governance, which has been in a state of decline, has been replaced by either a more private regulation or, in the case of corporations, self-regulation under the guise of being regulated.

> Since Keynes believed that a government that heavily regulated economic affairs could achieve optimal levels of wealth and employment, we credit him with the creation of *government capitalism*, where the government and

85 R. Edward Freeman et al., *Stakeholder Theory: The State of the Art* (Cambridge: Cambridge University Press, 2010), at 239.

86 R. Edward Freeman et al., *Stakeholder Theory: The State of the Art* (Cambridge: Cambridge University Press, 2010), at 251.

> its rights dominate the needs of all other stakeholders in the narrative of capitalism.[87]

This model is contrasted with a more investor-centric model.

> In Friedman's view shareholders who are better off will continue to invest in the market and produce better results for all. Friedman and those who give priority to the concerns of investors above and beyond the concerns of other stakeholders, subscribe to *investor capitalism*.[88]

Freeman argues that the problem is not capitalism itself, but rather how capitalism functions in today's society. This is similar to other scholars' views on the varieties of capitalism. More capitalism might actually be the solution.[89] This would encourage competition and force corporations to be more responsible and to drag the laggards along with the leaders.

> We sketch a new vision of capitalism–stakeholder capitalism – founded on libertarian and pragmatist lines . . . We argue that we do not need to justify capitalistic systems based on the outcome or the alternatives – the principles of capitalism are worthy goals in and of themselves.[90]

While the debate about capitalism and the true purpose and goals of capitalism continue to be debated, there is room for workers in the discussion. The role that workers play within capitalism and the role that workers play in the workplace itself are important areas of discussion.

Shareholder voice

To increase shareholder voice the increased use of proposals may be useful.

The work of Professor Janis Sarra at the Faculty of Law at the University of British Columbia seems promising in regards to strengthening CSR principles. In her article "The Corporation as Symphony: Are Shareholders First Violin or Second Fiddle?"[91] she argues for a greater voice for shareholders. Sarra advocates for greater shareholder involvement through using existing mechanisms such as proposals. At the same time, that shareholders' voice should be increased; to

87 R. Edward Freeman et al., *Stakeholder Theory: The State of the Art* (Cambridge: Cambridge University Press, 2010), at 271 (emphasis in original).

88 R. Edward Freeman et al., *Stakeholder Theory: The State of the Art* (Cambridge: Cambridge University Press, 2010), at 272 (emphasis in original).

89 Idea borrowed from Professor Dirk Matten in March 2013 at the CBERN conference.

90 R. Edward Freeman et al., *Stakeholder Theory: The State of the Art* (Cambridge: Cambridge University Press, 2010), at 280.

91 Janis Sarra, "The Corporation as Symphony: Are Shareholders First Violin or Second Fiddle?" *University of British Columbia Law Review* vol 36 (2003) pp. 403–442 at 9.

change the corporation too much would fundamentally alter the duties or Directors and Officers and change the shareholder role. While changes may be made, they should not necessarily be too grandiose and not too sudden. This is important as certain groups may hold one of these powers exclusively or there may be overlap.

Shareholders may be thought of as passive property holders. This may lead to questions about how much weight should be given to their position as passive property holders. According to Berle and Means, this passive nature of the shareholder posits that the protection they are accorded is not necessary as they are able to withdraw their investment if they are unhappy. Other stakeholders in the corporation are not as able to move away from or distance themselves from the corporation – e.g. workers. Why protect one group that is so easily able to remove their capital and invest elsewhere when there are other groups that are arguably more connected or intertwined with the corporation? While investors such as shareholders and bondholders are valuable, they are the only group that is of value and deserving of protection when the corporation faces a loss or is harmed in any manner. Deserving is a loaded term when stipulating that some groups are worthy of protection and others are not, but it makes sense to consider which groups are vulnerable and which are benefited.

Professor Aaron Dhir's article "Realigning the Corporate Building Blocks: Shareholder Proposals as a Vehicle for Achieving Corporate Social and Human Rights Accountability"[92] lays out numerous instances of shareholder proposals being used to address human rights/social policy (HRSP). While the research done by Dhir is related to my own research, his focus is not on labour standards but more broadly on CSR issues (human rights, environment, etc.) Also, his research does not employ empirical research, as it does not appear that he has looked to the actual text of shareholder proposals to study their impact. While he states that proposals are building blocks, the analogy does not ring true, as a corporation is more akin to a house and the tools (shareholder proposals) allow for the corporation to be remodelled or renovated to form a better structure while still essentially remaining the same structure, but improved. Shareholder proposals, while a vehicle for change, do not try to re-invent the entire structure but gradually and incrementally are able to effect change. Dhir looks to Talisman and Greenpeace, which are not labour-related cases.

Examining the correlation between corporate behaviour and underlying political systems is important. This is similar to Berle and Means's discussion of how capitalism allows corporations to even exist and states often allow for corporations to thrive. This is making use of the business case for CSR. However, the issue as to whether CSR is sincere or is window-dressing arises again. Does the motivation behind corporate behaviour matter? Whether corporations are

92 Aaron Dhir, "Realigning the Corporate Building Blocks: Shareholder Proposals as a Vehicle for Achieving Corporate Social and Human Rights Accountability" *ABLJ* vol 43 (2006) p. 365.

increasing social responsibility for "the good of society" or to increase profits may not be pertinent. As long as the result is the desired outcome, then perhaps the motive is irrelevant. Law does not exist in a vacuum and must be seen as realistic rather than abstract.

This is important as much as defining terms in scholarship is, as two people cannot engage in meaningful conversation without first understanding what they mean when speaking of such words as "justice" and "fairness" in regards to corporations and workers. And when one speaks of CSR in theory, how it plays out in the corporate realm is often rather different. Not all stakeholder groups are the same or have uniform interests. This is part of the complication: that what one group wants may not be the same as another, and within each of those groups there may not be consensus. CSR reporting is an area unto itself as the push to increase CSR is one part and the enforcement and compliance is yet another part. It is true that corporations are being regulated in a manner akin to self-regulation as the state does not have the resources to monitor on its own. This will be discussed further on in the book. The model of command and control is more antiquated in that regulation is more fluid currently. CSR is not completely without vulnerability in that the mechanisms set in place could possibly be co-opted, but the same can be said of the law itself.

Workers' rights

While I will explore all aspects of workers' rights in my review, I will not include anti-capitalist research. The work done by Professor Abigail Bakan[93] is useful in the broader debate but may be too tangential to my book. Many scholars, such as Professors David McNally and Leo Panitch,[94] lean towards changes in capitalism as being rather useless and that only through the overthrow of capitalism and implementation of socialism will workers gain true equality. These debates do involve workers' rights but are outside the scope of my book.

This literature discusses how activists and unions are helping to build the rights of workers of those that work in sweatshops. The general tone of the literature is one of sympathy for the workers and a desire to ease their abuse. Also, the investigation and monitoring of existing sweatshops and the drive to either put them out of business or force corporations to reform is often the mandate.

In her work,[95] Ethel Brooks provides information on the sweatshop free movement, which has gained momentum across university and college campuses throughout North America. The group "Students Against Sweatshops" which

93 Abigail Bakan & Eleanor MacDonald, eds., *Critical Political Studies: Debates and Dialogues from the Left* (Kingston: McGill-Queen's University Press, 2002).

94 See David McNally, *Another World Is Possible: Globalization and Anti-Capitalism* (Winnipeg: Arbeiter Ring Publishing, 2002).

95 Ethel Brooks, *Unraveling the Garment Industry: Transnational Organizing and Women's Work* (Minneapolis: University of Minnesota Press, 2007), at Back Cover.

sprang up across university and college campuses across North America can be credited with bringing more attention to the anti-sweatshop movement, alternatively called the "sweatshop free movement." Once a school implements a code of conduct, it is ensuring that items bearing the university's logo are made under fair working conditions. The university usually adopts a Code of Conduct, which governs the relationship between the university and its suppliers and sub-suppliers. While it is generally thought that sweatshops are a developing world problem, this is not true, as the working conditions even in certain parts of North America are horrendous. "The purpose of transnational protest is to connect corporate image with labor practices in order to improve the latter."[96] While sometimes activists in developed nations can lend their voice to those in developing nations, it must be noted that those trying to help must not force their values and ideals on to the others and have to avoid being paternalistic.

> When garment workers who are at the center of the transnational protest campaigns have been blocked from resolving their grievances, advocacy groups have stepped in and used their privileged networks, citizenship status, and access to language to carry out campaigns in support of labor rights.[97]

Some successful campaigns to be noted are "The National Labor Committee's 1995 campaign against Gap Inc."[98] and the Kathie Lee Gifford scandal of 1996.[99] Brooks notes that "American Apparel has made immense profit on its sweatshop-free branding, bringing in $250 million in sales in 2004. In 2003, however, UNITE HERE charged that American Apparel has been blocking the union from organizing in its factory."[100] American Apparel has drawn criticism as using whitewash to portray their company as socially responsible and sweatshop free, yet that image conflicts with an alternate image that has been developed in the media.

In their work, Archon Fung, Dara O'Rourke, and Charles Sabel[101] provide information about the anti-sweatshop movement. This material is useful for my book because the CSR debate encompasses the labour rights movement and the rights of workers more broadly. In their book, the authors "proposed a system

96 Ethel Brooks, *Unraveling the Garment Industry: Transnational Organizing and Women's Work* (Minneapolis: University of Minnesota Press, 2007), at Introduction XV.

97 Ethel Brooks, *Unraveling the Garment Industry: Transnational Organizing and Women's Work* (Minneapolis: University of Minnesota Press, 2007), at Introduction XVII.

98 Ethel Brooks, *Unraveling the Garment Industry: Transnational Organizing and Women's Work* (Minneapolis: University of Minnesota Press, 2007), at 27.

99 Kathie Lee Gifford was a TV talk show host who created a line of clothing for Wal-Mart, which was eventually linked to child labour abuses. This drove her to tears on her show and she became involved with campaigning for human rights.

100 Ethel Brooks, *Unraveling the Garment Industry: Transnational Organizing and Women's Work* (Minneapolis: University of Minnesota Press, 2007), at 167.

101 Archon Fung, Dara O'Rourke, & Charles Sabel, *Can We Put an End to Sweatshops?* (Boston: Beacon Press, 2001).

for corporate disclosure of information that would inform the public about corporate labor and environmental standards and, they hope, pressure companies to 'ratchet standards upward.'"[102] Contrasted with Kerr's seven principles of CSR,[103] they offer four. "Four principles – transparency, competitive comparison, continuous improvement, and sanctions – can guide activists, consumers, public officials, and managers in building an encompassing framework to organize these efforts."[104] The authors raise some interesting and important questions that are akin to playing the Devil's advocates. Should we be talking about rights or standards?[105] Should these rights/standards be regulatory or voluntary?[106]

While in law school, two other law students and I were successful in convincing Queen's University to adopt a Code of Conduct, ensuring that products made with the Queen's logo would be made under fair working conditions. This early venture into the anti-sweatshop movement was instrumental in fuelling my current research. Codes of conduct are important, but only through compliance and proper enforcement is the document to hold true force. "Students across the US have won public disclosure agreements from their administrations which require licensees to disclose factory locations. This relatively recent demand for public disclosure has been surprisingly successful (and would not have been predicted even two years ago)."[107]

Anti-sweatshop movement and supply chain management

In *The Travels of a T-Shirt in the Global Economy Second Edition: An Economist Examines the Markets, Power, and Politics of World Trade*, Pietra Rivoli attempts to study how the T-shirt she purchased at a store made its way around the world from China to the United States of America.

> In 2005, I met Dr. Dick Auld, a chaired professor of Plant Genetics and Breeding at Texas Tech. He had grown up on a cotton farm, and had memories of coming home from school and handpicking and handweeding, the endless hours of backbreaking labor in the merciless sun. "Why am I here today?" he asked rhetorically about his academic careers. "Why do I

102 Archon Fung, Dara O'Rourke, & Charles Sabel, *Can We Put an End to Sweatshops?* (Boston: Beacon Press, 2001), at foreward xi.

103 Michael Kerr, Richard Janda & Chip Pitts, *Corporate Social Responsibility: A Legal Analysis* (Toronto: LexisNexis Canada Inc., 2009).

104 Archon Fung, Dara O'Rourke, & Charles Sabel, *Can We Put an End to Sweatshops?* (Boston: Beacon Press, 2001), at 19.

105 Archon Fung, Dara O'Rourke, & Charles Sabel, *Can We Put an End to Sweatshops?* (Boston: Beacon Press, 2001), at 44.

106 Archon Fung, Dara O'Rourke, & Charles Sabel, *Can We Put an End to Sweatshops?* (Boston: Beacon Press, 2001), at 47.

107 Charles Sabel, Dara O'Rourke, & Archon Fung, "Ratcheting Labor Standards: Regulation for Continuous Improvement in the Global Workplace" on SSRN: <http://papers.ssrn.com/sol3/papers.cfm?abstract_id=253833>, at 25.

> keep doing the research? Because no human being should have to work that way, or live that way, not here, not anywhere, not ever again."[108]

The impact of Auld's experience working on such a farm really brings the human face into the research in that his experiences shaped his research and made him want to ensure that future farmers and farm workers do not have to battle under such conditions. The relationship between the corporations and the university was also discussed. For example, "the tractor-mounted cotton stripper [was] one of many applications of the fruitful relationship among USDA cotton researchers, universities, and farmers."[109] Wally Darneille, president of the Plains Cotton Cooperative Association in Lubbock, told the author, "'Farmers are the original environmentalists' . . . 'Telling a farmer to take care of the land is like telling the ice cream man to keep his freezer plugged in.'"[110]

Rivoli's analysis is similar to Bhagwati's in that they view the activists as ill-informed or uninformed.[111] Rivoli then goes on to write about the anti-sweatshop campaigns in the 1990s.

> In the mid-1990s, a variety of labor abuses came to light in factories that produced shoes and apparel for the Nike Corporation. Charges of underage workers, coerced or forced overtime, safety violations, and generally poor conditions began to surface, especially in factories in China and Indonesia. The factories, while supplying goods to Nike, were independently owned and operated. As a result, Nike argued, it bore no responsibility for conditions in its suppliers' factories.[112]

108 Pietra Rivoli, *The Travels of a T-Shirt in the Global Economy Second Edition: An Economist Examines the Markets, Power, and Politics of World Trade* (Hoboken: John Wiley & Sons, Inc., 2009), at 36.

109 Pietra Rivoli, *The Travels of a T-Shirt in the Global Economy Second Edition: An Economist Examines the Markets, Power, and Politics of World Trade* (Hoboken: John Wiley & Sons, Inc., 2009), at 37.

110 Pietra Rivoli, *The Travels of a T-Shirt in the Global Economy Second Edition: An Economist Examines the Markets, Power, and Politics of World Trade* (Hoboken: John Wiley & Sons, Inc., 2009), at 47.

111 See Pietra Rivoli, *The Travels of a T-Shirt in the Global Economy Second Edition: An Economist Examines the Markets, Power, and Politics of World Trade* (Hoboken: John Wiley & Sons, Inc., 2009), at 119: "But of all the rallying cries of the anti-globalization movement, the call to 'stop the race to the bottom' is both the scariest and the most nonsensical, especially when it comes from rich-country activists who owe their own prosperity to the very race they wish to halt for others. Who, we might ask, would these activists like to keep on the farm? Yet if some activists are misguided in their ideas about stopping the race to the bottom, others are a powerful force in changing the nature of the bottom itself."

112 Pietra Rivoli, *The Travels of a T-Shirt in the Global Economy Second Edition: An Economist Examines the Markets, Power, and Politics of World Trade* (Hoboken: John Wiley & Sons, Inc., 2009), at 125.

The notion of securing their supply chain to make sure that no products or elements of products be produced in sweatshops was a difficult task at first for many corporations. Later, when codes of conduct were implemented and monitoring agencies were signed on, the process would become more standard.

> The notion that apparel companies should be responsible for the conditions in their suppliers' factories – the so-called "supply chain" – was a novel and unwelcome idea to most companies. Indeed, the idea that a customer *could* be responsible for what happened behind the factory gates of its suppliers was unheard of.[113]

Corporate codes of conduct within the apparel industry forced a new standard upwards – that by one corporation signing on, other corporations felt pressure to do the same.

> As with the struggles over child labor or minimum wage, the idea that large corporations should be responsible for workplace practices in their supply chains went from radical notion to mainstream business practice. Corporate codes of conduct for suppliers to the footwear and apparel industry are nearly universal in the United States today, and the mainstream business press now routinely advises large companies on how to address labor conditions issues in Asia.[114]

This is particularly evident in the campus campaigns against sweatshops.[115] The notion of a monitoring agency quickly caught on with corporations and universities alike.

> Of course, the code carried little weight if it could not be monitored or enforced. By 2000, the Workers Rights Consortium (WRC) was founded

113 Pietra Rivoli, *The Travels of a T-Shirt in the Global Economy Second Edition: An Economist Examines the Markets, Power, and Politics of World Trade* (Hoboken: John Wiley & Sons, Inc., 2009), at 126.

114 Pietra Rivoli, *The Travels of a T-Shirt in the Global Economy Second Edition: An Economist Examines the Markets, Power, and Politics of World Trade* (Hoboken: John Wiley & Sons, Inc., 2009), at 126.

115 See Pietra Rivoli, *The Travels of a T-Shirt in the Global Economy Second Edition: An Economist Examines the Markets, Power, and Politics of World Trade* (Hoboken: John Wiley & Sons, Inc., 2009), at 127: "The students at Georgetown and elsewhere had a variety of demands: They wanted the companies that produced our T-shirts to disclose the names and addresses of the factories producing the clothing. They wanted the companies to adopt a strict code of conduct regarding factory conditions, and they wanted a system of independent monitoring in place that would check for compliance with the codes."
See also the work of Students Against Sweatshops in its various incarnations across North American campus. See also the work of what was formerly known as the Maquila Solidarity Network. See also the work of UNITE HERE and Oxfam.

> by international labor rights experts, universities, and students. Funded by member universities as well as outside sources, the WRC began to perform in-depth factory investigations for code-of-conduct compliance, and began to issue public reports containing its findings.[116]

The discussion has moved from occupying offices such as in the 1960s to a more civilized conversation in boardrooms in current times. The discussion has also moved from being consulted after the fact to having a seat at the table when decisions are being made – being part of the process rather than told what happened after.

"Hard law" versus "soft law"

It is important to look at those who make or implement laws and rules and those who have to comply. This can be termed "rule-maker versus rule-taker." The issues regarding whether there is a correlation between adherence to CSR initiatives and improved rights of workers in relation to stringent versus lenient codes, industry versus civil society codes, and independent verification versus self-verification are also examined. Also, the variance of rights is explored in regards to whether and how voluntary initiatives and official labour laws interact, etc.

In their edited work,[117] John Kirton and Michael Trebilcock define "soft law" as something that comes in many forms, "from private and voluntary codes and certification and labelling systems to transparency obligations on the part of governments."[118] The editors note that

> [i]n both theory and, over time, in practice, both hard law and soft law have distinct, if not always unique, advantages and disadvantages of their own. Hard law offers the legitimacy, the strong surveillance and enforcement mechanisms, and the guaranteed resources that soft law often lacks.[119]

116 Pietra Rivoli, *The Travels of a T-Shirt in the Global Economy Second Edition: An Economist Examines the Markets, Power, and Politics of World Trade* (Hoboken: John Wiley & Sons, Inc., 2009), at 129.

117 John Kirton & Michael Trebilcock, eds., *Hard Choices, Soft Law: Voluntary Standards in Global Trade, Environment and Social Governance* (Cornwall: Ashgate Publishing Limited, 2004).

118 John Kirton & Michael Trebilcock, eds., *Hard Choices, Soft Law: Voluntary Standards in Global Trade, Environment and Social Governance* (Cornwall: Ashgate Publishing Limited, 2004), at 10.

119 John Kirton & Michael Trebilcock, eds., *Hard Choices, Soft Law: Voluntary Standards in Global Trade, Environment and Social Governance* (Cornwall: Ashgate Publishing Limited, 2004), at 11.

Governance

Governance and regulation are important when discussing codes of conduct. The discussion about transnational governance figures prominently, as does the role of the state. The rise of the corporation can be viewed as infringing on the power of government. The globalization of the world may be deemed to be the Americanization of the world through products, media, etc. As discussed earlier, this may in fact be true. The erasing or lowering of borders has allowed for the expansion of corporations beyond domestic walls. This movement for citizens trying to gain rights does not necessarily coincide with those same citizens asking for increased regulation of corporations. This battleground may be less easy to win.[120]

The intersection of CSR and workers' rights

In "Corporate Social Responsibility and Workers' Rights,"[121] Professor Lance Compa, of Cornell University's School of Industrial and Labor Relations, makes a great attempt to summarize a complex debate about corporate social responsibility (CSR) and the broader debate about workers' rights. The debate surrounding the rights of workers is very broad as it spans across law, political science, philosophy, and industrial relations. This article argued that CSR has come to mean something different from the original definition. As the author notes, "I viewed corporate social responsibility and corporate codes of conduct as public relations maneuvers to pacify concerned consumers. Behind a façade of social responsibility, profits always trumped social concerns."[122] Corporations may rally around corporate social responsibility in order to appease the masses, and in recognition of the shift to ethical consumption. This may force corporations to put substance behind their claims to be socially responsible. Because consumers are becoming more knowledgeable about products, the demand for ethical products may put pressure on corporations to adopt the same. Compa credits Levi's and Reebok for adopting internal codes of conduct in the 1990s.[123] But he also notes that "[c]ompanies monitoring and enforcing their own codes of conduct led inevitably to charges that the fox was monitoring the henhouse."[124] This is also shown by such organizations as the Fair Labor Association (FLA),

120 For a greater discussion of governance models please see Vanisha H. Sukdeo, *Regulation and Inequality at Work: Isolation and Inequality Beyond the Regulation of Labour* (New York: Routledge, 2018), at 192.

121 Lance Compa, "Corporate Social Responsibility and Workers' Rights" online: <http://digitalcommons.ilr.cornell.edu/articles/183/>.

122 Lance Compa, "Corporate Social Responsibility and Workers' Rights" online: <http://digitalcommons.ilr.cornell.edu/articles/183/>, at 1.

123 Lance Compa, "Corporate Social Responsibility and Workers' Rights" online: <http://digitalcommons.ilr.cornell.edu/articles/183/>, at 4.

124 Lance Compa, "Corporate Social Responsibility and Workers' Rights" online: <http://digitalcommons.ilr.cornell.edu/articles/183/>, at 4.

which was essentially created by the U.S. government, so it is questioned as to whether it is as effective as it could be. These groups can be described as "seeking improvement and compliance, rather than cutting off business and hurting the workers they are trying to help."[125] The author concludes by noting that CSR is only part of the solution. "CSR can only create a stable foundation for workers' rights with two other legs: 1) strong laws strongly enforced by government authorities, and 2) strong, democratic trade unions where workers can improve conditions through self-organization and collective bargaining."[126]

Susan Boyd, Dorothy Chunn, and Robert Menzies[127] are a great resource because they frame the CSR debate across disciplines, not just within the legal context. This is useful because it is important to know what business academics, as well as those in the legal community, are writing about the CSR movement. "Adam Smith said the vile maxim of capitalists is 'everything for ourselves and nothing for anyone else.'"[128] This notion of greed being a driving force is studied more in business than in law. The impact of greed in the law should be a further topic of discussion, especially in the realm of corporate crime.

> For people concerned to see the end of corporate abuse of working people, many aspects of consumer campaigns are appealing. First, such campaigns expose how corporate giants such as Nike are involved in an international chain of exploitation and hold them responsible for the labour practices of their contractors.[129]

Ratcheting labour standards

This seminal article by Sabel, O'Rourke, and Fung sets out a system that would increase the rights of workers. This system would help build up labour rights from more basic to more advanced.

> Globalization itself has freed capital from many of its former constraints – national workplace standards, collective bargaining, and supervisory state agencies and courts – designed to humanize working conditions. A natural response, best expressed in the ILO's core labor standards, has been to attempt to build global versions of national institutions by establishing

125 Lance Compa, "Corporate Social Responsibility and Workers' Rights" online: <http://digitalcommons.ilr.cornell.edu/articles/183/>, at 5.
126 Lance Compa, "Corporate Social Responsibility and Workers' Rights" online: <http://digitalcommons.ilr.cornell.edu/articles/183/>, at 6.
127 Susan Boyd, Dorothy Chunn, & Robert Menzies, eds., *[Ab]Using Power: The Canadian Experience* (Halifax: Fernwood Publishing, 2001), at Back Cover.
128 Susan Boyd, Dorothy Chunn, & Robert Menzies, eds., *[Ab]Using Power: The Canadian Experience* (Halifax: Fernwood Publishing, 2001), at 26.
129 Susan Boyd, Dorothy Chunn, & Robert Menzies, eds., *[Ab]Using Power: The Canadian Experience* (Halifax: Fernwood Publishing, 2001), at 156.

> universal minimum standards of work and international inspectorates and courts to monitor and enforce them.[130]

Private regulation beyond the model of state-centred regulation has allowed for greater flexibility in corporate response. Codes of conduct are one vehicle among many.

> We offer "Ratcheting Labor Standards" (RLS) as a regulatory strategy that does just this; rather than devising institutions that attempt to constrain the rapidly changing forces and processes of globalization, RLS attempts to redirect some of these energies toward the advancement of social ends.[131]

This RLS model that the authors devised does not set out a regulatory framework or a way of making the theory practical. "First, it [RLS] would require *every* firm in a regulated sector (e.g., apparel or footwear) to adopt *some* certified provisions for monitoring their labor standards performance."[132] This notion of an industry-wide standard is worth pursuing, as then one is comparing like with like rather than trying to transcribe norms from one industry to another. "At this early stage, interested parties might best proceed by grasping the basic principles of RLS and then reflecting upon its merits and implications for their own strategies."[133] The authors outline that RLS will create competition between companies to become leaders as opposed to laggards.[134]

Sabel, O'Rourke, and Fung go on to state that unscrupulous companies may adopt a code and then find "pliant monitors" to attest to the corporation's sincerity. The authors do not attack codes of conduct in and of themselves but look past that to argue that codes could be misused. They appear to deride the use of codes of conduct unnecessarily. "As a transparent and encompassing

130 Charles Sabel, Dara O'Rourke, & Archon Fung, "Ratcheting Labor Standards: Regulation for Continuous Improvement in the Global Workplace" on SSRN: <http://papers.ssrn.com/sol3/papers.cfm?abstract_id=253833>, at 1.

131 Charles Sabel, Dara O'Rourke, & Archon Fung, "Ratcheting Labor Standards: Regulation for Continuous Improvement in the Global Workplace" on SSRN: <http://papers.ssrn.com/sol3/papers.cfm?abstract_id=253833>, at 1.

132 Charles Sabel, Dara O'Rourke, & Archon Fung, "Ratcheting Labor Standards: Regulation for Continuous Improvement in the Global Workplace" on SSRN: <http://papers.ssrn.com/sol3/papers.cfm?abstract_id=253833>, at 2 (emphasis in original).

133 Charles Sabel, Dara O'Rourke, & Archon Fung, "Ratcheting Labor Standards: Regulation for Continuous Improvement in the Global Workplace" on SSRN: <http://papers.ssrn.com/sol3/papers.cfm?abstract_id=253833>, at 3.

134 "Unlike a fixed-rule regime, which aims to ensure that all facilities exceed minimum thresholds, RLS establishes an on-going competition in which laggards pursue leaders and leaders attempt to out-do themselves because they know that no particular level confers ascendancy." Charles Sabel, Dara O'Rourke, & Archon Fung, "Ratcheting Labor Standards: Regulation for Continuous Improvement in the Global Workplace" on SSRN: <http://papers.ssrn.com/sol3/papers.cfm?abstract_id=253833>, at 2.

knowledge-base, RLS would enable trade unions to enhance their own knowledge of best labor practices world-wide and to constantly update that knowledge as new trends emerge in sectors or regions."[135] Sabel, O'Rourke, and Fung do not construct an actual model but describe what a potential model might entail – strong monitoring and enforcement of a standard that is set across an industry. This is distinct from the model I envision, because I do not see the need for industry-wide agreement. Rather, I conceive of individual corporations choosing to adopt a code of conduct for its own purposes – whether that is to appease consumers and potential consumers, shareholders, stakeholders, etc. The differing pressures on individual corporations allow for it to choose which code of conduct is best suited to its needs and whether it chooses to focus on workers' rights, environmental concerns, etc. This may depend on the industry. In the apparel industry, workers' rights and environmental concerns may both be important; but perhaps in the farming industry, environmental concerns are paramount. Allowing each individual corporation to choose its code also allows for a higher level of malleability and direct reflection of the workplace rather than importing outsider codes.[136]

Reflexive labour law

Simon Deakin's work on reflexive labour law outlines how labour and employment law has been changed by the internationalization of work.[137] Because labour has been outsourced to other nations, the home nation is able to avoid regulation at the same standard and seek out other places to have goods sourced and manufactured where the labour laws are more lax.

Self-regulation

As mentioned earlier in this chapter, we need to explore the role of government in relation to stakeholder theory, as the state-centred model of governance has been replaced by a more private regulation, or self-regulation under the guise of being regulated in the case of corporations.

Gunningham and Rees outline the difference between self-regulation by individual organization versus self-regulation in groups, as once the regulation involves more than one entity, it becomes more akin to industry-wide

135 Charles Sabel, Dara O'Rourke, & Archon Fung, "Ratcheting Labor Standards: Regulation for Continuous Improvement in the Global Workplace" online: <http://papers.ssrn.com/sol3/papers.cfm?abstract_id=253833>, at 35.

136 Employee protection can be ensured by having workers on the committee that chooses the standard to be implemented. While there is always the threat that workers can be swayed by management such a threat always exists.

137 See Simon Deakin and Ralf Rogowski, "Reflexive Labour Law, Capabilities and the Future of Social Europe" available on SSRN.

regulation.[138] "It is necessary to distinguish between individual self-regulation (where an entity regulates itself, independent of others) and self-regulation by groups."[139] The authors go on to state that true self-regulation rarely exists, as most forms of self-regulation involve governmental action and can be thought of as co-regulation instead of self-regulation.[140] "One can distinguish forms of self-regulation in terms of the degree of government involvement (for as we shall see, 'pure' self-regulation, without any form of external intervention, is very uncommon)."[141] The form of regulation can be thought of as spanning a wide array of forms such as in hard law and soft law – the variety within these forms is vast.

Professor Harry Arthurs notes that corporations superseding their reach through self-regulation is not new but is rather antiquated and a return to the old, as he cites the examples of the Hudson's Bay Company and East India Tea Company as enormously powerful corporations that were almost state-like.[142] Rather than corporation-centred regulation being novel, it is in fact long-standing.

Self-regulation can be described as governing internal behaviour and can include such aspects as ethics and morality to alter behaviour. Perhaps one is more inclined to abide by a code of conduct when one thinks that some underlying moral code is at play. "Moreover, because self-regulation contemplates ethical standards of conduct which extend beyond the letter of the law, it may significantly raise standards of behaviour."[143] This interconnection of ethics, morality, and the law is apparent in *BCE*, as the SCC holds that there is a new standard of a good corporate citizen. The word "good" alone is tied to ethics and morality. The word "citizen" connotes a sense of duty and responsibility towards both country and fellow citizens. It also implies rights and privileges flowing from the country to its citizens.

In line with the Law and Economics school, the argument can be made that taxpayer money should not be used to regulate corporations when the

138 Neil Gunningham & Joseph Rees, "Industry Self-Regulation: An Institutional Perspective" *Law and Policy* vol 19 no 4 (Oct. 1997) pp. 363–414.

139 Neil Gunningham & Joseph Rees, "Industry Self-Regulation: An Institutional Perspective" *Law and Policy* vol 19 no 4 (Oct. 1997) pp. 363–414 at 364.

140 See, for example, even the Law Society of Upper Canada, a self-regulating body that governs lawyers in Ontario. It gets its jurisdiction from legislation which is obviously governmental. See also page 400 of Gunningham and Rees: "It is often crucial that self-regulation operates in the shadow of rules and sanctions provided by the general law, for it is these which are the most obvious and visible (but not the only) means of giving regulates the incentive to comply with the self-regulatory program."

141 Neil Gunningham & Joseph Rees, "Industry Self-Regulation: An Institutional Perspective" *Law and Policy* vol 19 no 4 (Oct. 1997) pp. 363–414 at 365.

142 Harry W. Arthurs, "Private Ordering and Workers Rights in the Global Economy: Corporate Codes of Conduct as a Regime of Labour Market Regulation" (2002) Osgoode Digital Commons Paper 15, online: <http://digitalcommons.osgoode.yorku.ca/scholarly_works/15>, at 475.

143 Neil Gunningham & Joseph Rees, "Industry Self-Regulation: An Institutional Perspective" *Law and Policy* vol 19 no 4 (Oct. 1997) pp. 363–414 at 366.

corporations can regulate themselves. Why not allow corporations to fund their own regulation without burdening taxpayers? Self-regulation may be an alternate way to switch the cost to corporations and allow the government to remain to be seen as neutral in this regard. Governments are able to avoid being labelled as pro-corporation or anti-corporation by standing by as spectators rather than actors in regard to corporate regulation. It is a very neoliberal argument that taxes should not be allocated for anything beyond the most basic of services; but in regard to the regulation of corporations, perhaps the best way forward is to allow those who are best able to understand corporate needs be left to those who are internal to the corporation itself.

Examples such as the business judgment rule show that when the government, through the courts, is willing to allow corporations to decide what the best "business decisions" are by giving deference to Directors and Officers' decision-making in regard to what is best for the business. The government should allow corporations to self-regulate because they may be the entities best positioned to regulate effectively. The problems of governmental regulation can be linked to the resources available to those departments and then to the judges making the decisions about the complicated business transactions.

This movement from nation state as the fundamental source of authority has given way to the corporation as a new form of governance. The rise of the corporation and the power and wealth contained therein allow the corporate form to dominate on the world stage. This rise in power can be attributed to both the acquiescence of the governments to voluntarily give up power and, at the same time, the corporations actively seizing power.

Transnational governance models have resulted in less state power. The positives gained through globalization may be outweighed by the negatives gained at the same time. "There is no clear dichotomy between self-regulation on the one hand and government regulation on the other. Rather, there is a continuum, with pure forms of self-regulation and government regulation at opposite ends."[144] Governmental action is behind so much of the ability to self-regulate. One can self-regulate only with governmental permission or the absence of governmental control in that area. Only where there is a governance void can space be occupied for self-regulation.

> Notice first how the term industry "self-regulation" is a little deceptive. When we look closely at the leading examples of industry self-regulation (including health care), we see that they involve varying degrees of interaction with government regulation, a symbiosis that influences the dynamics of industry self-regulation in important ways.[145]

144 Neil Gunningham & Joseph Rees, "Industry Self-Regulation: An Institutional Perspective" *Law and Policy* vol 19 no 4 (Oct. 1997) pp. 363–414 at 366.

145 Neil Gunningham & Joseph Rees, "Industry Self-Regulation: An Institutional Perspective" *Law and Policy* vol 19 no 4 (Oct. 1997) pp. 363–414 at 398.

Private regulation

Private regulation is used to describe non-state regulation and governance. Distinct from self-regulation, where the entity uses internal mechanisms to regulate, private regulation involves an outside source that is non-governmental. This external source ensures compliance and may include external monitoring. This operates outside of legislation and other hard law mechanisms. Sabel, O'Rourke, and Fung[146] describe this as a way of "ratcheting labour standards" (RLS) without the use of hard law. Allowing labour standards to be strengthened outside of state governance is to allow private actors to set the terms of their own relationships. This may lead to a more interactive and fulfilling model of governance between the parties. However, in the alternative this may allow for even floor-level standards to be undercut. What becomes the floor and what becomes the ceiling on labour rights? Also, private regulation can lead to what I term "consumer regulation." This is the government downloading their responsibilities pertaining to regulation on to consumers, so that consumers themselves regulate which products are able to be on the market.

Current Canadian scheme

Legislative scheme

Government
↓
Employer ↔ Employees

The current scheme that protects the rights of workers in Canada is Employment Law, which is individual employees having a contract with their employer. In the Canadian context, each province or territory has its own provincial legislation that covers basic employment rights in the workplace such as working hours, overtime payment, etc. In Ontario, the *Employment Standards Act*[147] (*ESA*) and other statutes guarantee certain working conditions for workers.

The unionized workplace

Government (and private arbitration)
↓
Employer ↔ Employees (and the Union)

146 Charles Sabel, Dara O'Rourke, & Archon Fung, "Ratcheting Labor Standards: Regulation for Continuous Improvement in the Global Workplace" online: <http://papers.ssrn.com/sol3/papers.cfm?abstract_id=253833>.

147 *Employment Standards Act, 2000*, SO 2000, c. 41.

Another form of regulation in Ontario (and other jurisdictions) is Labour Law, which is the unionized workplace where the employer and employees have a collective agreement (CA) that governs the conditions of the workplace. Every CA in Canada incorporates the *ESA* as basic conditions and cannot be contracted out of unless it is "a greater benefit." The Ontario *Labour Relations Act, 1995*[148] sets out when disagreements can be sent to the Ontario Labour Relations Board, which gets its power from the statute.

International scheme

International law → individual employers

International Law, including the UN ILO Conventions, lays out basic minimums for workers. However, unless those rules and regulations are enacted in domestic law, they are unenforceable in Canadian courts.

My research looks at how to increase the rights of workers in the era of union decline (see the decline of the auto industry in North America) and attaches responsibility to the corporation itself, which forces the corporation to abide by the code of conduct no matter what jurisdiction. Many sources, such as shareholders, activists, NGOs, etc., put pressure on the Corporation to adopt a code of conduct which guarantees certain working conditions. The arrow points both ways between the corporation and employees because there are obligations that flow from the employee to the employer. In the unionized context, the employees also have the Union on their side; but in the scheme I develop, the employees are alone. There is no "protection" beyond the code and its internal resolution procedure. The code may be enforced by an external monitoring agency such as the Fair Labor Association (FLA) or Workers Rights Consortium (WRC), but they are not really "protection" for the worker in the same way that the Union is in the unionized setting. The code of conduct is somewhat similar to the CA in Labour Law but does not have the power of the state to enforce, like the role of the Ontario Labour Relations Board, etc. This is what takes the rights of workers into the realm of soft law, unlike Labour Law. This model is able to be adopted in workplaces where unionizing is difficult.

The model I envision

Shareholders →
Activists → Corporation ↔ employees
NGOs →

The model I envision is one in which some shareholders, activists, and NGOs put pressure on the Corporation to reform itself. The Corporation then enacts

148 *Labour Relations Act, 1995*, SO 1995, c. 1, Sched. A.

a code which has obligations flowing both ways between the Corporation and its employees. This attaches duties to the Corporation directly rather than have duties imposed upon the Corporation from the government or other external sources. This code would be enforced through an external monitoring agency to ensure compliance.

Monitoring agency
↓
Corporation ↔ employees

Creating documents that govern workplace environments that allows for the incorporation of the workers' voices may allow for a more fulsome model of governance – one in which the governed help to develop the terms that govern their working environment.[149] Allowing labour standards to be strengthened outside of state governance is to allow private actors to set the terms of their own relationships. This may lead to a more interactive and fulfilling model of governance between the parties. Without a legislative framework that guarantees some basic level then the minimum (or floor) can drop for those acting outside a legislative framework. The notion that workers are crafting their own workplace rules is not that far removed from the area of collective agreements however codes of conduct can be developed in places that are not unionized (and places where unionization may be quite difficult).[150] While it may be the case that NGOs drive the change, the employees are allowed to be involved in the process in a way that the process of drafting legislation does not allow. Greater worker voice can be included in a process that is not driven by management – even if employees are not the main drivers.

Activists and targets

Activists can choose which entity (or entities) to target in order to effect change. This can be thought of as activists first targeting individual corporations in order to get that specific corporation to change its behaviour. In the alternative, or at the same time, activists can work towards getting an industry-wide standard enacted or a code of conduct in place. Third, at the same time as the other options or viewed as a higher level target, activists can target the government to change corporate laws or other rules to bring about change.

149 This may be akin to the German model, where Boards are often composed of workers to the limit of 50% worker representation.

150 This model may prove useful in jurisdictions where union-busting still occurs. In places where union organizers still face the threat of violence and reprisal, union building is difficult, and this model may prove easier to implement because it happens at the top of the organization rather than from the bottom up in the case of union organizing.

Textbox 1.1 Activists and targets (1)

1) Activists targeting one corporation
2) Activists trying to implement industry-wide standards or code of conduct
3) Activists targeting government

Textbox 1.2 Activists and targets (2)

Activists target consumers
Consumers impact change on corporation
Corporation changes as a result of consumers (not activists)

In another way of conceptualizing the targets, activists can target consumers to raise awareness about which corporations are operating sweatshops and to try to change that behaviour. In that approach, the activists are using the consumers as a gateway to change behaviour. If the corporation responds to the consumers' demands, then the corporate behaviour will change. This uses the consumers as a conduit to bring about change through the activists' information sharing. "As actors in and representative of a world culture, transnational activists can draw on the substantial argumentative resources of being disinterested, 'rationalized' others."[151]

The current task for my research is to blend together the rather divergent literature on CSR and workers' rights to mould it into a proper foundation for my book. There are many gaps in the literature, so my research will fill in those gaps to demonstrate how CSR is able to further the rights of workers. True CSR will enable positive changes, so the task before me is how to measure CSR and determine the corporations that are truly practicing it and those who are merely pretending.

Bibliography for Chapter 1

Legislation

Canada *Business Corporations Act*, R.S.C. 1985, c C-44, s. 122.
Employment *Standards Act*, SO 2000, c 41.
Labour *Relations Act*, SO 1995, c 1, Sched. A.

151 Brian Holzer, *Moralizing the Corporation: Transnational Activism and Corporate Accountability* (Northampton: Edward Elgar Publishing Limited, 2010), at 5.

Caselaw

BCE Inc v 1976 Debentureholders, 2008, SCC 69.
Chevron Corp v Yaiguaje, 2015, SCC 42.
Choc v Hudbay Minerals Inc, 2013, ONSC 1414.
Peoples *Department Stores v Wise*, 2004, SCC 68.
Secondary sources

Books

Bakan, Abigail & Eleanor MacDonald, eds., *Critical Political Studies: Debates and Dialogues from the Left* (Kingston: McGill-Queen's University Press, 2002).

Berle, Adolf A. & Gardiner Means, *The Modern Corporation and Private Property* (New York: The MacMillan Company, 1932).

Bhagwati, Jagdish, *In Defense of Globalization* (New York: Oxford University Press, 2007).

Brooks, Ethel, *Unraveling the Garment Industry: Transnational Organizing and Women's Work* (Minneapolis: University of Minnesota Press, 2007).

Boyd, Susan, Dorothy Chunn, & Robert Menzies, eds., *[Ab]Using Power: The Canadian Experience* (Halifax: Fernwood Publishing, 2001).

Crane, Andrew et al., *The Oxford Handbook of Corporate Social Responsibility* (Oxford: Oxford University Press, 2008).

Ellis, Mark, *Fiduciary Duties in Canada, Looseleaf* (Toronto: Carswell, 2011).

Freeman, R. Edward et al., *Stakeholder Theory: The State of the Art* (Cambridge: Cambridge University Press, 2010).

Fung, Archon, Dara O'Rourke, & Charles Sabel, *Can We Put an End to Sweatshops?* (Boston: Beacon Press, 2001).

Heal, Geoffrey, *When Principles Pay: Corporate Social Responsibility and the Bottom Line* (New York: Columbia University Press, 2008).

Holzer, Brian, *Moralizing the Corporation: Transnational Activism and Corporate Accountability* (Northampton: Edward Elgar Publishing Limited, 2010).

Kerr, Michael, Richard Janda, & Chip Pitts, *Corporate Social Responsibility: A Legal Analysis* (Toronto: LexisNexis Canada Inc., 2009).

Kirton, John & Michael Trebilcock, eds., *Hard Choices, Soft Law: Voluntary Standards in Global Trade, Environment and Social Governance* (Cornwall: Ashgate Publishing Limited, 2004).

McNally, David, *Another World Is Possible: Globalization and Anti-Capitalism* (Winnipeg: Arbeiter Ring Publishing, 2002).

Mitchell, Lawrence E., *Corporate Irresponsibility: America's Newest Export* (New Haven: Yale University Press, 2001).

Pava, Moses L. & Joshua Krausz, *Corporate Responsibility and Financial Performance: The Paradox of Social Cost* (Westport: Quorum Books, 1995).

Rivoli, Pietra, *The Travels of a T-Shirt in the Global Economy Second Edition: An Economist Examines the Markets, Power, and Politics of World Trade* (Hoboken: John Wiley & Sons, Inc., 2009).

Sisodia, Rajendra, David B. Wolfe, & Jagdish N. Sheth, Firms of Endearment: How World-Class Companies Profit from Passion and Purpose (Philadelphia: Wharton School Publishing, 2007).

Sukdeo, Vanisha H., *Regulation and Inequality at Work: Isolation and Inequality Beyond the Regulation of Labour* (New York: Routledge, 2018).

Visser, Wayne et al., *The A to Z of Corporate Social Responsibility: A Complete Guide to Concepts, Codes and Organisations* (West Sussex: John Wiley & Sons Ltd, 2007).

Zadek, Simon, *The Civil Corporation* (London: Earthscan, 2007).

Articles

Arthurs, Harry W. "Private Ordering and Workers Rights in the Global Economy: Corporate Codes of Conduct as a Regime of Labour Market Regulation" (2002) *Osgoode Digital Commons* Paper 15 online: <http://digitalcommons.osgoode.yorku.ca/scholarly_works/15>.

Berle, Adolf A., "For Whom Corporate Managers Are Trustees: A Note" *Harvard Law Review* vol 45 no 8 (June 1932) pp. 1365–1372.

Carroll, Archie, "A Three-Dimensional Conceptual Model of Corporate Performance" *The Academy of Management Review* vol 4 no 4 (October 1979) pp. 497–505.

Carroll, Archie, "Corporate Social Responsibility: Evolution of a Definitional Construct" *Business & Society* vol 38 no 3 (September 1999) pp. 268–295.

Coase, Ronald, "The Nature of the Firm" *Economica* vol 4 no 16 (November 1937) pp. 386–405.

Compa, Lance, "Corporate Social Responsibility and Workers' Rights", online: <http://digitalcommons.ilr.cornell.edu/articles/183/>.

Deakin, Simon & Ralf Rogowski, "Reflexive Labour Law, Capabilities and the Future of Social Europe" available on SSRN: < https://papers.ssrn.com/sol3/papers.cfm?abstract_id=1780922>.

Dhir, Aaron, "Realigning the Corporate Building Blocks: Shareholder Proposals as a Vehicle for Achieving Corporate Social and Human Rights Accountability" *ABLJ* vol 43 (2006) p 365.

Dodd, E. Merrick, "For Whom Are Corporate Managers Trustees?" *Harvard Law Review* vol 45 no 7 (May 1932) pp. 1145–1163.

Friedman, Milton, "The Social Responsibility of Business Is to Increase its Profits" in *The New York Times Magazine*, September 13 1970.

Goodpaster, Kenneth E., "Business Ethics and Stakeholder Analysis" *Business Ethics Quarterly* vol 1 no 1 (January 1991) pp. 53–73.

Gunningham, Neil & Joseph Rees, "Industry Self-Regulation: An Institutional Perspective" *Law and Policy* vol 19 no 4 (October 1997) pp. 363–414.

Sabel, Charles, Dara O'Rourke, & Archon Fung, "Ratcheting Labor Standards: Regulation for Continuous Improvement in the Global Workplace" on SSRN: <http://papers.ssrn.com/sol3/papers.cfm?abstract_id=253833>.

Sarra, Janis, "The Corporation as Symphony: Are Shareholders First Violin or Second Fiddle?" *University of British Columbia Law Review* vol 36 (2003) pp. 403–442.

Utting, Peter, "Corporate Responsibility and the Movement of Business" *Development in Practice* vol 15 no 3/4 (June 2005) pp. 375–388.

Vogel, David, "Private Global Business Regulation" *Annual Review of Political Science* vol 11 (2008) pp. 261–282.

Waitzer, Edward & Johnny Jaswal, "Peoples, BCE, and the Good Corporate 'Citizen'" *Osgoode Hall LJ* (2009) pp. 439–496.

Zumbansen, Peer & Simon Archer, "The BCE Decision: Reflections on the Firm as a Contractual Organization" (2008) *Comparative Research in Law & Political Economy*. Research Paper No 17/2008, online: <http://digitalcommons.osgoode.yorku.ca/clpe/191> at 9–10.

Websites

Harvard Kennedy School of Government, online: <www.hks.harvard.edu/m-rcbg/CSRI/init_approach.html>.
Maquila Solidarity Network, online: <http://en.maquilasolidarity.org/resources/video/StopSweatshops>.

2 Codes of conduct

I analyse corporate codes of conduct by industry leaders which also employs a rigourous monitoring process in accordance with its code of conduct. I also analyse the empirical research done by scholars on the efficacy of codes once implemented. Codes of conduct operate on a spectrum, as one code can be weak and ineffectual and another can be so strict that it rivals hard law. The implementation of the code is important, as the actors who are involved in the drafting process can be CEOs or simply the lawyers. It is important to note who is at the table during the process and who is left out. Enforcement of the code usually involves a monitoring agency in place of the government in regard to hard law. I will examine competing monitoring agencies to determine which is most impactful. The compliance with the code is yet another issue to encourage corporations to comply before there is a breach. Once a breach occurs, there must be a remedy to deal with future behaviour. These steps mimic hard law but go beyond hard law, because the process is more malleable to accommodate and fit with differing corporations. Rather than accept hard law as a blunt tool with no room for flexibility, the code of conduct can be unique to each workplace/corporation and be tailor made to fit the needs of both the corporation and the worker. Similar to how differing workplaces choose to organize with a specific union in the unionized context, so too can workplaces have different codes of conduct.

My methodological approach uses empirical data compiled by scholars who have travelled to Mexico, China, and India to conduct their research. That work was conducted by speaking with factory workers in the varying jurisdictions. Many rights in Canada are bestowed or granted by the government, rather than fought for through citizen action like the American Revolution and that more violent past versus Canadian independence from England. It is often thought that Canadian history is less radical and less violent, but I think it is important to highlight a rather neglected part of Canadian labour history such as the Winnipeg General Strike.[1] From the radical roots of the

1 For a greater discussion of the Winnipeg General Strike, please see Vanisha H. Sukdeo, *Regulation and Inequality at Work: Isolation and Inequality Beyond the Regulation of Labour* (New York: Routledge, 2018), at 18–32.

Winnipeg General Strike, Canadian workers gained rights through legislation like the *Employment Standards Act* and the *Ontario Labour Relations Act.* The difference between unionized workers and non-unionized workers seems to be ever growing as benefits granted to full-time workers get left out of benefit packages for part-time workers. So from workers gaining rights embedded in legislation, whether they are unionized or not, to the gig economy, we see the regression yet again of workers' rights. How has the law changed in response to the emergence of the gig economy? Slowly, as the decisions surrounding the gig economy have indicated. There are also decisions in the U.K. about Uber as well as in Seattle. Again, the assistance that gig workers need might be found in a code of conduct. This is malleable and can fit any workplace, unlike legislation. Legislation can be amended to fit an individual workplace, but it is unlikely. A code can be changed more easily; however, it does not mean that it will be. This still allows more power to workers to gain control of their workplace governance. A code bridges isolation and inequality in a way that legislation does not, and cannot. This is the difference between those who act within the corporation – shareholders and employees – versus those who are external – community members like in *Choc* and *Chevron.* The law has changed to bring in more stakeholders, and the Court has adopted some of the Ruggie Report to hold corporations accountable, but more needs to be done. The law will continue to change, and it could align more with CSR principles and move towards stakeholder theory being actualized. I bring the concept of alienation into the corporate law discourse in a way that is unique. I attempt to normalize Marxist critiques of the corporation – even within my Business Associations classroom while I teach.

While workers have seen an increase in basic rights such as wage increases and shorter working hours, the rise of technology has led to a corresponding "disruption" of work itself. In my other research, I discuss how labour platforms such as Uber have led to less stable work – work that is piecemeal and precarious. I devise a model that I term "wavering work."

I then examine how corporate law can be used to help increase the rights of workers. I discuss codes as well as suggest amendments to the *Canada Business Corporations Act.* Changing both hard law and soft law will allow for changes to happen simultaneously, rather than choose to focus on only one option. Both my hard law suggestions plus codes focus on the corporation as a site of power.

My methodology included research using books, journals, and websites. For the gig economy, I drew data from the McKinsey Report as well as Prassl's work. There are not many scholars, as it is a new mode of work. This is also a big disruption in work. Some even say that this is the biggest change since the Industrial Revolution. The Industrial Revolution moved work from the home into factories. And we can see with the gig economy that there is now regression back from a separate and distinct workplace that workers travelled to every single day towards back to work being centred at home – using one's own car for Uber, or working from home.

I compiled a set of 30 codes of conduct from an earlier set that flowed from shareholder proposals that dealt with labour-related issues. After studying those 30 different codes and coding them from easy to hard and from lax to strict, I selected three rigourous codes to build my own and included the Queen's Code as well. Where is my own Model Code on this spectrum from lax to strict? I would say that it is stricter than lax and very much mirrors hard law enforcement mechanisms.

After analysing the different codes I offer my own Model Code of Conduct in the book. I have built on the code from my other work.[2] This allows for management to have a template available to build on. I rely on empirical research conducted by scholars to best develop a strong and reasonable code of conduct. If the code offered is too strict, management may decline to adopt it so it is best to reach a reasonable code that is neither too weak nor too strict, that will be adopted, and that can be built on in the future. My Model Code includes various amended sections from the different codes I have studied. I adapted the most suitable parts and created my own code.

A good starting point is to have a code implemented and then continue to build on that code in the future. The code, once adopted, can be flexible to adapt to the individual workplace in a way that hard law cannot. In that regard, soft law can be more responsive and adaptable than hard law. Mamic terms this the feedback loop, where once a code is implemented, it can be assessed by a third party such as a monitoring agency as well as by those who enforce it like management and those who are "ruletakers" such as the workers whose work is governed by the code.

The initial stage is the drafting and creation of the code. Then the code has to be implemented. As outlined by Mamic, the implementation of a code will vary from place to place. The corporation may already have an ethics code or employee code of conduct which dictates employee behaviour, which is distinct from my Model Code. As noted by Mamic and Locke, it is important that a code is able to be amended to change with the corporation itself. As can be noted in hard law, when a new government comes into power, they can easily repeal legislation that was enacted by the previous government. So it is not as though legislation is everlasting. Once a code is in place and able to be adaptable, it is important to ensure compliance and provide for enforcement of the code with a monitoring agency.

2 Please see Vanisha H. Sukdeo, *Regulation and Inequality at Work: Isolation and Inequality Beyond the Regulation of Labour* (New York: Routledge, 2018), at 251.

Shareholder-focused governance

Expanding the fiduciary duty in the corporate law context will ultimately dilute the duty. So perhaps there can be another way to increase protection for workers within corporate law through a more stakeholder-focused version of corporate law theory. The shareholder primacy model is akin to shareholder dominance because the theory states that shareholders will be given the utmost importance when corporate decisions are made. Perhaps it is time to replace the shareholder primacy model not with stakeholder theory but with a shareholder-focused model that allows shareholders to be lowered from the level in shareholder primacy but not so low as to be considered directly alongside stakeholders. This model of shareholder-focused governance would allow for the theory to be described more broadly as placing shareholders at the forefront, but not the only interests that count.

This movement from shareholder wealth maximization and/or the shareholder primacy model can move into the shareholder-focused model, then onwards to stakeholder theory actualized. This would allow for a smoother transition from rather divergent models that of shareholder primacy and stakeholder theory to have a bridging model that allows for laws to be changed without being drastic.

Shareholder primacy model → shareholder-focused model
→ stakeholder theory actualized

This allows for corporate culture to change to keep pace with the law. Also, elements can be added in slowly and allow for everyone to adapt rather than a sudden shift from one model to another. *Peoples* and *BCE* have helped to usher in this new model, which is not exactly as I have described. This transition model that I am describing does not describe the current Canadian landscape. Elements would need to be changed.

The divergent paths of corporate law and labour law

The theory that corporations are simply a nexus of contracts means that there are individual contracts acting upon each person that intersects with other contracts.

> In the corporate nexus, there are two main kinds of contracting parties: the "fixed claimants," who specifically negotiate the terms of each contract they have with others in the firm, and the "residual claimants" who do not negotiate each term, but rely upon a standard statutory structure to define their rights and obligations."[3]

3 Peer Zumbansen & Simon Archer, "The BCE Decision: Reflections on the Firm as a Contractual Organization" (2008) Comparative Research in Law & Political Economy.

If you do not have a binding contract like the bondholders with the corporation, then you are left to hold residual rights found in legislation or at common law – such as employment law. This relegates those without a formal contract to second class citizens who are not afforded the degree of rights and claims as those with contracts. The equality of this argument is to be tested by various theorists as those who do not have contracts may be less sophisticated and suffer as a result of their lack of power, etc.

In corporate governance, the Board of Directors of a corporation is elected by the shareholders of the corporation. The duties of the Board include the hiring and firing of Executives, executive compensation, and decisions about dividends to be paid out to shareholders. The Board has the task of making sure that the interests of shareholders are protected. The Chief Executive Officer (CEO) is the highest ranking executive in a company, and the CEO's duties include managing the overall operations of a company and being the conduit between the Board and operations. The CEO may be responsible for the generation of revenue for the corporation as well as creating strategic and financial plans, developing goals, and acting as a liaison to the public, government, etc. There is also the position of Chief Financial Officer (CFO), whose primary responsibilities are managing the financial risks of the corporation. The CFO reports directly to the CEO. The CFO may have duties involving the preparation of financial statements on a quarterly basis, budgetary planning, revenue trends, financial record keeping, etc. The Chief Operating Officer (COO) is responsible for the operations management and for seeing that the CEO's plans and strategies reach fulfilment. The Chief Technology Officer (CTO) is a position that may be found at technology-based corporations such as Facebook and Google.

According to Canadian law, a corporation must exist with a "view to a profit"; whether a profit is actualized is a separate issue. These three basic business associations (sole proprietor, partnership, and corporation) are for-profit ventures which are distinct from charities and not-for-profits (formerly called non-profits).

Table 2.1 Different business associations

1. Sole proprietor	Wholly liable for a business
2. Partnership	A group of individuals joined together to run a business
General	
Limited Liability	
3. Corporation	A separate legal person from the individuals who run the corporation – be it directors, officers, etc.
Private	
Public	

Research Paper No 17/2008, online: <http://digitalcommons.osgoode.yorku.ca/clpe/191>, at 9–10.

Besides the three typical ways of carrying on a business (sole proprietor, partnership, and the corporation) note that there exist between those models other less utilized models such as the cooperative,[4] benefit corporation,[5] and community contribution companies[6] (in British Columbia) and the Community Interest Company (CIC) in the U.K.

Origins of the corporation and the corporate shield

The Salomon Principle is derived from a 19th-century U.K. case, *Salomon v Salomon & Co Ltd.*,[7] which states that the corporation is a separate legal entity from its shareholders, Directors, and Officers. This gave rise to the term "the corporate veil" which allows for shareholders, directors, and officers to gain protection from liability by being separate from the corporation itself. The legal distinction between the corporation and its Directors and Officers is important, because without that separation, the Directors and Officers could be personally liable for the debts and expenses of the corporation. Contrasted with the Directors and Officers of a corporation, sole proprietors are completely responsible for the businesses they run. So the corporate form allows for a shield to be in place between those who work for the corporation and the corporation itself. One can see the evolution from sole proprietor to partnership and on to the corporate form.

Salomon is a U.K. case so it is important to note that it has to be adopted into Canadian law by a Canadian decision that cites to it. It is common in the Canadian legal landscape for courts to look to the U.K. and the U.S.A. for decisions that rule on similar legal issues. Canadian law is very much informed and influenced by U.K. law, but recall that the laws in the U.K. are not binding on Canadian courts. So only when a Canadian court has imported a U.K.

4 A Cooperative ("coop") is a business or enterprise, owned by a group of persons seeking to satisfy common needs. Contrasted with the for-profit and not-for-profit corporations, coops may pay their surplus to members in the form of patronage returns. A coop can be incorporated either with or without membership shares.

5 See Vanisha H. Sukdeo, "What Is the Benefit of a 'Benefit Corporation'?: Examining the Advantages and Detriment" *Banking and Finance Law Review* vol 31 no 1 (2015) pp. 89–111: "A Benefit Corporation ('BC') is a new corporate form that outlines obligations beyond shareholder wealth maximization developed in the United States of America ('U.S.') that is intended to make corporations more socially responsible. The organization B Lab certifies socially responsible corporations that they term 'B Corporations' or 'B Corps.' This voluntary certification scheme is distinct from BCs established under statute. The first state to pass BC legislation was Maryland in April 2010. Vermont was second in May 2010. There are commonalities among the legislation as all four deal with 'general public benefit,' 'specific public benefit' and require a 'third party standard.' There are differences in the wording but the underlying premise is the same."

6 For more information about community contribution companies please see Vanisha H. Sukdeo, "What Is the Benefit of a 'Benefit Corporation'?: Examining the Advantages and Detriment" *Banking and Finance Law Review* vol 31 no 1 (2015) pp. 89–111.

7 *Salomon v Salomon & Co Ltd.* [1897] AC 22.

decision into Canadian law by citing its principles does that law from another country become part of Canadian law. In the Canadian case of *Macaura v Northern Assurance Co Ltd.*[8] it was held that in order to have an insurable interest in property, a person must have a legal interest in said property. Note that *Salomon* is an 1897 decision and *Macaura* is a 1925 decision. In the lifetime of caselaw, this is a small gap, so it can be inferred that the outcome in *Macaura* was influenced by the *Salomon* decision.

Fiduciary law informs how fiduciaries must fulfil their obligations and what punishment will result in the failure to perform. As noted by Waitzer and Sarro,

> [a]s a result, fiduciary law effectively places the onus on fiduciaries to reflect on their legal relationships and consider how to act in accordance with these duties. Fiduciaries that ignore this onus risk having standards of appropriate conduct articulated for them after the fact.[9]

While the extent of the duty may be vague, it is useful for the fiduciary to understand their role from the forefront and to recall that they are required to put the beneficiary's needs above all others. This is sometimes difficult to execute, but the area is so narrow and the duty so importantly held that there should be corresponding importance given to the weight and severity of the duty before accepting it. One who accepts a fiduciary duty towards another is doing so freely and should properly inform themselves about what the duty entails and what is required to properly fulfil the duty. It is not to be enter into lightly.

BCE further informs us that pension plans hold tremendous power in society including large amounts of capital for investment. "Fiduciaries charged with managing and advising investment vehicles that encompass multiple generations of beneficiaries, like pension plans, must therefore consider the intergenerational implications of their decisions (or advice)."[10] The duty towards future generations is often discussed in the Aboriginal Law area because of the need to consider how to preserve culture and a certain way of life from one generation to another. The duty to future generations is often discussed in the Environmental Law because of the need to reduce pollution so that future generations can live in a world that has not been ravaged by climate change. The fact that corporate law mist consider future generations through way of decisions made by pension plan board members is novel. But it is true. If board members of pension plans must weigh business decisions while considering future generations it moves the conversation from one of short term gain to long term gain to very long term gain. When one considers future generations how far into

8 *Macaura v Northern Assurance Co Ltd.* [1925] AC 619.

9 Ed Waitzer & Douglas Sarro, "Fiduciary Society Unleashed: The Road Ahead for the Financial Sector" *The Business Lawyer* vol 69 (Aug. 2014) at 1091.

10 Ed Waitzer & Douglas Sarro, "Fiduciary Society Unleashed: The Road Ahead for the Financial Sector" *The Business Lawyer* vol 69 (Aug. 2014) at 1096.

the future must one look? One hundred years from today? Or one thousand years from today?

Waitzer and Sarro go on to note that fiduciary law will change in the future. They term this an ethical fiduciary which seems similar to a more principles-based approach to law, where the rule and the underlying rationale behind the rule must be followed. This is contrasted with the typical rules-based approach to law, where the rule must be followed without necessarily looking behind the rule to determine the reasoning that led to the rule.

> First, the fiduciary of the future will need to be an ethical fiduciary: one that recognizes and follows through on its responsibility to preserve and build on the institutional system in which the fiduciary is embedded, and on which the fiduciary relies.[11]

This is a more holistic approach, and one that works well with the *BCE* decision's advances towards stakeholder theory and taking a "big picture" analysis of where corporate law fits and how corporate governance decision-making should be made in light of the expansion of duties, perhaps even fiduciary duties. Placing the corporation and corporate decisions within the landscape and space of broader society allows for greater emphasis to be placed on how those decisions impact everyone within society and not just shareholders. This will lead to a more fulsome model of corporate governance. This also allows for space that was once exclusively corporate to be infiltrated by the needs of other groups. This may lead to too many needs to be considered, but it is a balancing act to figure out whose interests matter and whose interests takes priority within the decision-making process.

Amendments to the *CBCA*

Possible new amendments to section 122 of the *CBCA* are as follows (amendments appear in bold):

122. 1 Every director and officer of a corporation in exercising their powers and discharging their duties shall

a act honestly and in good faith with a view to the best interests of the corporation **including in order of priority: shareholders, employees, suppliers, creditors, consumers, governments, and the environment**; and

b exercise the care, diligence, and skill that a reasonably prudent person would exercise in comparable circumstances.

11 Ed Waitzer & Douglas Sarro, "Fiduciary Society Unleashed: The Road Ahead for the Financial Sector" *The Business Lawyer* vol 69 (Aug. 2014) at 1098.

Duty to comply

2 Every director and officer of a corporation shall comply with this Act, the regulations, articles, by-laws and any unanimous shareholder agreement.

No exculpation

3 Subject to subsection 146(5), no provision in a contract, the articles, the by-laws or a resolution relieves a director or officer from the duty to act in accordance with this Act or the regulations or relieves them from liability for a breach thereof.[12]

I transplanted the language from paragraph 42 of *Peoples* to make the words not just within the decision but also contained within the legislation. It is important to note that the second group after shareholders is employees. I agree that employees are the second-most important group after shareholders, and there are obligations to employees already codified in the legislation about being able to go after directors for unpaid wages. Employees do not occupy the essential position that shareholders do, but they are a very important part of the corporation. See the work of Professor Richard Locke and his conclusions about the two factories in Mexico, one in which employees were given greater input into the workplace and allowed to have a voice within the process, and one in which employees did not have such an option. The workplace where workers were happier and engaged had a higher output level. Also worth noting is that some employees also do wear two hats of being an employee and a shareholder because of employee stock option plans.

One other point about the amendments is that the list detailed in *Peoples* included "governments," as did I; however, it might be quite circular for the government to have legislation that is altered to create a duty to the government itself. My suggested amendments, quite in line with *Peoples* and *BCE*, included governments, and I do not see much of a problem with the language, but I wanted to address what might be deemed problematic.

Amending the *CBCA* is also helpful overall beyond *BCE* compliance, as the entire statute could be revised to be more in line with stakeholder theory and CSR values more broadly. This would help align the legislation with the changing values of society. Shareholder wealth maximization is the antiquated approach to corporate law, and stakeholder theory actualized is the progressive approach.

Amendments to the CBCA to incorporate the language from Peoples will allow the law to be more uniform. Clear language is better than uncertain terms. The legislation would be clear about who owes the duty and to whom the duty is owed. This expansion on caselaw and common law becoming legislated is

12 Some language from *Canada Business Corporations Act*, RSC 1985, c C-44 at s 122. Amendments in bold.

useful, as having such language in legislation may make it more difficult for the new duties to be overturned by a new case. Having language from caselaw be codified into legislation gives it greater clarity, as the legislature is able to debate legislation before it gets enacted in a way that caselaw is not able to. Judges hand down decisions at the trial level by themselves, and only at the appellate and Supreme Court levels do judges decide alongside other judges. This lack of opportunity for consultation before deciding may in fact be limiting in a way that appellate level courts are not. This may seem like a minor issue, but having judges decide by themselves may leave too much discretion in the hands of a lone judge.

My code includes basic rights like working hours as well as advanced rights like organizing.

He goes on to state that codes are viewed as undemocratic, lack the power of the state to enforce, and party specific so they benefit only a small group.[13]

What are the basic provisions which should be included in all codes? As indicated in the chart detailing the comparison of the three there are some areas that should be covered in all codes (Table 2.4). Number 11 is an advanced right of freedom of association and collective bargaining. Number 12 and 13 are more about enforcement and compliance. There should be a preamble outlining the purpose of the Code. A preamble is used in all three codes, and they are sufficient.

Shareholder primacy model

Corporations can still take various forms under shareholder primacy model as described by numerous theorists. The corporation is not one single form and static. In 1932 Dodd stated that there are leaders and laggards regarding corporate governance leadership. "The principal object of legal compulsion might then be to keep those who failed to catch the new spirit up to the standards which their more enlightened competitors would desire to adopt voluntarily."[14] This seems akin to CSR theory, which posits that there are leaders and laggards in regards to CSR corporate leaders which draw in the laggards to compete with more socially responsible companies. Dodd goes on to discuss corporate philanthropy, which is still debateable whether that is in fact CSR, but it does run against agency theory in the construct that the corporation is to serve the best interests of the shareholders.[15] Unless the business case for CSR is used, this may lead to the thinking that by making corporate donations it may increase profit in the long term.

13 Larry Cata Backer Blog Post on Sep. 21, 2013, online: <http://lcbackerblog.blogspot.ca/2013/09/changing-corporate-behavior-through.html>.

14 E. Merrick Dodd, "For Whom Are Corporate Managers Trustees?" *Harvard Law Review* vol 45 no 7 (May 1932) pp. 1145–1163 at 1153.

15 E. Merrick Dodd, "For Whom Are Corporate Managers Trustees?" *Harvard Law Review* vol 45 no 7 (May 1932) pp. 1145–1163 at 1158.

Kenneth Goodpaster notes that

> [m]anagers who would pursue a multi-fiduciary orientation for their companies must face resistance from those who believe that a strategic orientation is the only *legitimate* one for business to adopt, given the economic mission and legal constitution of the modern corporation.[16]

Goodpaster is taking exception to the shareholder primacy model, which states that shareholders are the only concern for Directors when making decisions. Rather, Goodpaster offers that there might be other non-fiduciary relationships beyond the fiduciary duty to shareholders.[17]

Carroll describes "social responsiveness" as the philosophy behind business' response to social responsibility.

> Social responsiveness can range on a continuum from no response (do nothing) to a proactive response (do much). The assumption is made here that business does have a social responsibility and that the prime focus is not on management accepting a moral obligation but on the degree and kind of managerial action.[18]

This is important because if it is accepted that corporations *do* have a duty to society at large then the next question is about what kind of duty that would be (how rigourous or lax the duty will be).

Shareholder proposals

Shareholder proposals are but one part of the CSR umbrella, in that they serve as a mechanism to increase the responsibility of corporations. The interesting aspect of shareholder proposals in that they are an internal mechanism to effect change. The corporation has instruments within itself to remodel or renovate its structure. Shareholder proposals allow shareholders to have voice, which is important in the same way that worker voice is important – the fact of being heard is valued in and of itself. The *CBCA*[19] Section 137 outlines the applicable

16 Kenneth E. Goodpaster, "Business Ethics and Stakeholder Analysis" *Business Ethics Quarterly* vol 1 no 1 (Jan. 1991) pp. 53–73 at 63.

17 Kenneth E. Goodpaster, "Business Ethics and Stakeholder Analysis" *Business Ethics Quarterly* vol 1 no 1 (Jan. 1991) pp. 53–73 at 69–70: "Management may never have promised customers, employees, suppliers, etc. a 'return on investment,' but management is nevertheless obliged to take seriously its extra-legal obligations not to injure, lie to or cheat these stakeholders *quite apart from* whether it is in the stockholders' interests."

18 Archie Carroll, "A Three-Dimensional Conceptual Model of Corporate Performance" *The Academy of Management Review* vol 4 no 4 (Oct. 1979) pp. 497–505 at 501.

19 *Canada Business Corporations Act*, R.S.C. 1985, c. C-55.

laws that govern shareholder proposals. Subsection 137 (1.1)[20] outlines the criteria that the person(s) submitting the proposal must meet. If the proposal is submitted by someone who does not meet the criteria in subsection 137 (1.1), the corporation may refuse to include the proposal under subsection 137 (5.1) .[21] The proposal might be added by management in any event on the basis of the results of their independent research and the public reaction to the issues. A company might think it is best to let the shareholders ultimately decide what direction the corporation should be taking in regards to the company's connection to certain products. "[I]n the aftermath of Enron-type scandals, faced with an increase in the frequency of shareholder proposals and majority votes, boards have become significantly more responsive to shareholder resolutions."[22] Shareholders are concerned with stock prices, and lower consumer support may result in lower stock prices and thus lower value for their investment.

When management's research coincides with the shareholder proposal, it bodes well as both management and the shareholders may more easily agree upon the direction taken.

> Some shareholder activity has also focused on human rights issues and a push for greater transparency in corporate decision-making in respect of foreign labour practices. A recent proposal regarding sweatshop employment practices garnered 36% of shareholder support at the corporation's annual meeting, the largest vote ever recorded in support of a social resolution submitted to a Canadian corporation.[23]

Other cases involving shareholder proposals are making management aware of the impact of consumers and their increasing demand for corporate responsibility in the area of fair labour standards. "The rate of implementation [of shareholder

20 *Canada Business Corporations Act*, R.S.C. 1985, c. C-55, subsection 137 (1.1) states: "To be eligible to submit a proposal, a person (a) must be, for at least the prescribed period, the registered holder or the beneficial owner of at least the prescribed number of outstanding shares of the corporation; or (b) must have the support of persons who, in the aggregate, and including or not including the person that submits the proposal, have been, for at least the prescribed period, the registered holders, or the beneficial owners of, at least the prescribed number of outstanding shares of the corporation."

21 *Canada Business Corporations Act*, R.S.C. 1985, c. C-55, subsection 137 (5.1) states: "If a person who submits a proposal fails to continue to hold or own the number of shares referred to in subsection (1.1) up to and including the day of the meeting, the corporation is not required to set out in the management proxy circular, or attach to it, any proposal submitted by that person for any meeting held within the prescribed period following the date of the meeting."

22 Yonca Ertimur, Fabrizio Ferri, & Stephen R. Stubben, "Board of Directors' Responsiveness to Shareholders: Evidence from Shareholder Proposals" online: <www.hbs.edu/research/pdf/08-048.pdf>, at 1.

23 Janis Sarra, "The Corporation as Symphony: Are Shareholders First Violin or Second Fiddle?" *University of British Columbia Law Review* vol 36 (2003) pp. 403–442 at 9.

proposals] has increased dramatically after 2002, doubling to more than 40%."[24] This increase in the success of shareholder proposals bodes well for increased shareholder voice while at the same time increasing accountability to shareholders and other stakeholders.

However, when an individual or an organization has a personal stake in a shareholder proposal, the proposal should be drafted to make it seem impartial. Unions such as the National Union of Public and General Employees (NUPGE) are involved in a campaign against Wal-Mart; however, the rules against "acting in the best interests of the corporation" force them to cloak their true motives. "Great pains must be taken to ensure that the proposal speaks to how the issue, despite being political or social in nature, primarily relates to the corporation's business."[25] It may be found that a proposal can be blocked under subsection 137 (5), which states:

> 137 5 A corporation is not required to comply with subsections (2) and (3) if
>
> b it clearly appears that the primary purpose of the proposal is to enforce a personal claim or redress a personal grievance against the corporation or its directors, officers or security holders;
>
> b.1 it clearly appears that the proposal does not relate in a significant way to the business or affairs of the corporation;
>
> . . .
>
> e the rights conferred by this section are being abused to secure publicity.

Shareholder proposals also advance the interests of other stakeholders. Shareholders are likely most concerned about their shares gaining value; however, due to the increased ability of consumers to make known their preference for socially conscious products and services, corporations that do not follow this CSR-driven course are losing money as a result of their refusal to become more socially aware. At the end of the day, in adapting to consumers' demands for social awareness and the lack of consumer support for products not made under fair working conditions, corporations should amend their labour policies otherwise they may face lower share prices.

The rules for shareholder proposals are not fair and reasonable, as the threshold requirements under subsection 137 (1.1) are onerous. If a shareholder does not have the required amount of shares their voice is silenced. "In order to

24 Yonca Ertimur, Fabrizio Ferri, & Stephen R. Stubben, "Board of Directors' Responsiveness to Shareholders: Evidence from Shareholder Proposals" online: <www.hbs.edu/research/pdf/08-048.pdf>, at 2.

25 Aaron A. Dhir, "Realigning the Corporate Building Blocks: Shareholder Proposals as a Vehicle for Achieving Corporate Social and Human Rights Accountability" *ABLJ* vol 43 (2006) p. 365 at 395.

submit a proposal under the revised legislation, shareholders must own either 1% of total outstanding voting shares on the date of submission, or own shares that have a fair market value of at least $2,000 at the close of business on the day before submission."[26] The denial or exclusion of a shareholder proposal does not have many avenues for recourse. "[I]f a shareholder wishes to dispute management's decision to exclude a proposal, it has no recourse but to seek review in court."[27]

In the United States of America, the governing legislation is the *Securities Exchange Act* of 1934. Rule 14a-8[28] sets out the regulations that govern shareholder proposals in the U.S., which are similar to the provisions in the Canadian *CBCA*.

Corporations as citizens

Good corporate citizen" as defined by the SCC creates a new legal concept that is not defined in statute. Where are those governed by the CBCA and corporate governance to look to find the standard for what constitutes a "good corporate citizen"?

Professor Andrew Crane[29] outlines the definitions of key terms in the CSR debates. Also, he draws attention to certain changes that have been made in society that were not imagined, i.e. hybrid cars. The impact of consumer pressure for certain items is also explored, i.e. free range eggs after abuses of chickens at certain farms were exposed. Whether these changes to corporate behaviour are a result of external pressure (consumers, etc.) or internal (shareholders) is worthy of examination. Professor Crane also notes the emergence and popularity of products that are ethical/environmental i.e. Toyota Prius and Ben & Jerry's among others.[30]

Governance gap? Or governance gaping hole?

Let us consider how corporate governance can be improved for workers' rights as an example. While legislative changes and stronger laws in other countries may be the best approach and the most stringent with the power of the state

26 Aaron A. Dhir, "Realigning the Corporate Building Blocks: Shareholder Proposals as a Vehicle for Achieving Corporate Social and Human Rights Accountability" *ABLJ* vol 43 (2006) p. 365 at 385–386.

27 Aaron A. Dhir, "Realigning the Corporate Building Blocks: Shareholder Proposals as a Vehicle for Achieving Corporate Social and Human Rights Accountability" *ABLJ* vol 43 (2006) p. 365 at 399.

28 17 CFR § 240. Rule 14a-8 (2007).

29 Andrew Crane et al., *The Oxford Handbook of Corporate Social Responsibility* (Oxford: Oxford University Press, 2008).

30 Andrew Crane et al., *The Oxford Handbook of Corporate Social Responsibility* (Oxford: Oxford University Press, 2008), at 288.

behind such laws, there are ways that legislation can be hard to implement: (1) it is difficult to get new laws passed, (2) it is time consuming, (3) laws can be repealed, and (4) laws need an enforcement mechanism. First, passing news laws involves tabling bills, then having them pass through readings and then get implemented and out into force. Laws are of the utmost importance, but when the goal is to strengthen rights in other nations because they produce goods for the Canadian market, then strengthening Canadian laws will not have the desired impact. Even if laws are strengthened in Thailand and Honduras, they may not be strongly enforced. Second, the time it takes for a Bill to become law is time consuming. In order to effect change as quickly as possible, it may be easier to get the corporation to adopt a code which can take less time. A corporation can make that decision quite quickly and does not have to go through the lengthy process like a Bill does.

Third, even if a law gets passed, it can get repealed. This may seem like a simple argument to make in that anything that can be changed can be changed back, but it is important to recognize that laws do not necessarily last forever. Laws can be repealed, and it may be less likely that a code of conduct, an internal mechanism, gets removed than for a law to get repealed. The abolition of a law is also outside the power of the corporation, and it is impacted without any say. The decision to remove a code of conduct may be met with resistance by those internal to the corporation, be it customers, shareholders, etc. A current example is PETA buying shares of Canada Goose when it went public – the purpose was to try to get Canada Goose to stop using coyote fur on its coats. A group such as that shareholder group will protest and try to stop any internal changes to the corporation.

Fourth, in order for a law to be effective, it needs a strong enforcement mechanism. A law on the books that is not well enforced is not useful. So, the task is not just to get a law implemented, but to make sure that there are governmental resources enough to pay for the enforcement of the law. In the code of conduct context, the corporation has to pay for the monitoring agency so no government resources are used.

Corporate codes of conduct (also referred to as "codes of conduct") outline duties and responsibilities that flow from the corporation to stakeholders (employees, customers, etc.). These codes can be narrow in scope (ex. dealing only with environmental issues) or broad in scope (ex. environmental, labour, and social issues). The codes can be superficial or multifaceted. A more fulsome code would be broad in scope and quite detailed in regard to the language of the code itself and compliance mechanisms. A rather shallow code would be narrow in scope and use language that is vague and non-specific; perhaps such a code would be void of an enforcement mechanism. Codes can be internal, external, or third-party codes. The compliance and enforcement mechanisms used to monitor the code can also be weak or strong, or somewhere along the continuum. Bondy, Matten, and Moon note that code characteristics can be sorted as follows: (1) specific versus general, and that model codes contain more sweeping language, (2) comprehensive versus selective, as multi-stakeholder codes tend to be more comprehensive and include a broader set of issues, (3) positive versus negative in that some codes may be more principles-based while others are more rules-based and include language that is negative about what companies should abstain from doing, (4) voluntary versus mandatory, which is self-explanatory, and (5) equilegal versus supralegal as to what codes reflect existing laws and which move beyond minimal requirements.[31]

Codes also flow through different disciplines from law and business to political science. Who drafts the code (the rulemaker), and who is regulated by it (the ruletaker)? Whose voice is heard, and whose voice is silenced? How much influence, if any, does the voice of the worker have on codes? As Locke notes, "[w]e found that the opportunity to participate in decisions related to work process had a strong and positive effect on work climate."[32]

Empirical studies

Richard Locke

The work of Professor Richard Locke of MIT in studying the effectiveness of codes is very helpful in this research. Locke was able to personally attend numerous factories with his graduate students and conduct interviews with various stakeholders, including workers, and management. Professor Locke's research was conducted between 2005 and 2010 and included factories in Mexico, Bangladesh, China, Vietnam, Honduras, India, and Thailand.[33] While it seemed like Locke commenced his research with optimism that codes of conduct would help to improve working conditions for workers in the developing world, he completed his research with a different point of view. Locke found that due to the complexity of supply chains, it is difficult to make sure that every stage in the process is in compliance with the code. Also, he notes that different factories have different environments, so even in a direct comparison between two factories in Mexico producing goods for the same company, there are different interpretations of how to comply with the code. Management at one factory made workers work individually, while the other used groupwork. Management at one factory allowed for workers to have input in their workplace, while the other was more command and control with no input from workers. Locke concludes his book with the statement that labour rights can "only be promoted

31 Krista Bondy, Dirk Matten, & Jeremy Moon, "Codes of Conduct as a Tool for Sustainable Governance in MNCs" in S. Benn & D. Dunphy (eds.), *Corporate Governance and Sustainability: Challenges for Theory and Practice* (London: Routledge, 2006), at 14–15.

32 Richard M. Locke, *The Promise and Limits of Private Power: Promoting Labor Standards in a Global Economy* (New York: Cambridge University Press, 2013), at 110.

33 Richard M. Locke, *The Promise and Limits of Private Power: Promoting Labor Standards in a Global Economy* (New York: Cambridge University Press, 2013), at 22.

in our global economy through a mix of both private and public regulation."[34] While this may seem obvious, it really does demonstrate the limits of so-called "private power" which codes of conduct might rightfully be labelled. Only through coordination between governments and corporations can true effects be made in the fight to increase the rights of workers. Some work by its very nature is dangerous, such as mining, but rights can be put in place to ensure that safety precautions are ratified so that dangerous work is made less so.

> Throughout most of the twentieth century, labor standards were regulated largely on a national basis, through a mixture of laws, union-management negotiations, and company policies. Internationally, the conventions and technical services of the ILO provided an additional source of moral authority and advice but lacked significant enforcement power. The emergence of global supply chains, however, has rendered these national and international strategies inadequate because authority is dispersed not only across national regimes but also among global buyers and their myriad suppliers. It is in this context that private initiatives have emerged to fill this regulatory void.[35]

This movement from state-centred regulation to a more private-centred and corporation-centred mode of governance leaves open gaps to be filled in. While it is expected that state-centred regulation has many levels of government to ensure that all concerns can be addressed from federal to provincial to municipal, the regulation of a corporation does have that corresponding level of detail.

> The underlying assumption of this model of "private voluntary regulation" is that information collected through factory audits will be used both by labor rights NGOs and consumer groups to exert pressure on global brands to reform their sourcing practices as well as by the brands themselves, who rely on this information to police and pressure their suppliers into improving standards in their factories.[36]

34 Richard M. Locke, *The Promise and Limits of Private Power: Promoting Labor Standards in a Global Economy* (New York: Cambridge University Press, 2013), at xi: "Through an analysis of several private voluntary initiatives promoted by global corporations, lead suppliers/contract manufacturers, labor-friendly nongovernmental organizations (NGOs), and international organizations such as the International Labor Organization (ILO), this book sheds light on both the promise and the limitations of private power in enforcing labor standards for the millions of people employed in global supply chains. The central finding of this book is that working conditions and labor rights can only be promoted in our global economy through a mix of both private and public regulation."

35 Richard M. Locke, *The Promise and Limits of Private Power: Promoting Labor Standards in a Global Economy* (New York: Cambridge University Press, 2013), at 9.

36 Richard M. Locke, *The Promise and Limits of Private Power: Promoting Labor Standards in a Global Economy* (New York: Cambridge University Press, 2013), at 24.

To prove causation would be difficult; however, Locke notes that workplaces where there is greater collaboration did have higher outputs, lending support to the theory that a workplace with greater space for worker voice is more productive. This links with the discussion about naming, shaming, and blaming as well as my discussion about ethical consumption.

Locke began his research into working conditions by focusing on Nike and its promises to get rid of the use of sweatshops while at the same time making its reputation better.

> As early as the 1980s, Nike was criticized for sourcing its products in factories and countries where low wages, poor working conditions, and human rights problems were rampant. Then, over the course of the 1990s, a series of public relations nightmares-involving underpaid workers in Indonesia, child labor in Cambodia and Pakistan, and poor working conditions in China and Vietnam – tarnished Nike's image. As Phil Knight lamented in a May 1998 speech to the National Press Club, "The Nike product has become synonymous with slave wages, forced overtime, and arbitrary abuse."[37]

Nike has become quite the beacon for criticism from activists about the use of sweatshops in manufacturing products, and perhaps even the poster child for sweatshops.

Locke concludes his research on the factory as follows:

> [W]e analyzed the results of ABC's own audit data for the 210 factories that ABC reported to the FLA and were actively producing for ABC in May 2006. Out of these 210 factories, only 51 (24 percent) were in full compliance with the company's Code of Conduct. Another 53 percent of these suppliers were explicitly "not approved," and 22 percent were categorized as either "in progress" or "requiring follow-up," meaning that some combination of "terminal," "significant," and/or "minor flaws," as described by the company's auditing protocol, were found during the audit, and thus, the factory should be placed on hold – not allowed to produce for ABC – until these issues were rectified.[38]

Locke notes that

37 Richard M. Locke, *The Promise and Limits of Private Power: Promoting Labor Standards in a Global Economy* (New York: Cambridge University Press, 2013), at 49.

38 Richard M. Locke, *The Promise and Limits of Private Power: Promoting Labor Standards in a Global Economy* (New York: Cambridge University Press, 2013), at 41. Please note that Locke has used ABC to hide the true name of the company.

> [i]n summary, whereas the private compliance model assumes that working conditions in supplier factories can improve through a combination of audits and threats, our field research at the suppliers of several major global brands, competing in different industries and operating across the globe, illustrates the empirical weaknesses of these assumptions. In the private compliance model, accurate information collected through independent auditors informs global brands where to place their orders, and how best to reward (or punish) their suppliers for their compliance with the Code of Conduct.[39]

Locke concludes with a less optimistic take on the value of codes of conduct in advancing the rights of workers, since this "order placing power" does not seem to have been exercised. While suppliers who run afoul of the code can be punished through the cancellation of contracts, this may not actually be done. It seems as though there is a way to get suppliers to be in compliance with the code, but it may rarely be used and might in fact be a hollow threat. These deficiencies that he notes can be remedied, as he states that management needs to be trained to know the contents of the codes and how to properly ensure compliance. Problems such as these can be remedied by hosting training sessions to make sure that management knows the contents of the codes.

Locke, Rissing, and Pal outline that due to the absence of "strong national enforcement, a range of private regulatory efforts (i.e. codes of conduct, monitoring programmes, certification schemes, etc.) have emerged to address labour and environmental issues."[40] Where there is a governance gap, the corporation will be allowed that space to self-regulate. In the absence of an alternative, the corporation has to create its own system of accountability. Only with external pressure will such a regulatory plan gain strength. The true target of the activist power is sometimes difficult to determine – whether to target the retail store, the company head office, or elsewhere. The target is difficult to pinpoint, as sometimes factories make products for a number of corporations and may be subjected to varying standards.

> Some factories complain of "monitoring fatigue," given that they are monitored multiple times a year on behalf of each of the global brands they work for. In addition, suppliers complain of being placed in "compliance limbo" between different and conflicting code requirements.[41]

39 Richard M. Locke, *The Promise and Limits of Private Power: Promoting Labor Standards in a Global Economy* (New York: Cambridge University Press, 2013), at 38.

40 Richard M. Locke, Ben A. Rissing, & Timea Pal, "Complements or Substitutes? Private Codes, State Regulation and the Enforcement of Labour Standards in Global Supply Chains" *British Journal of Industrial Relations* vol 51 no 3 (Sep. 2013) pp. 519–552 at 520.

41 Richard M. Locke, Ben A. Rissing, & Timea Pal, "Complements or Substitutes? Private Codes, State Regulation and the Enforcement of Labour Standards in Global Supply

The work of other scholars

Judge Helen Keller, formerly of the University of Zurich, Faculty of Law and now a Judge at the European Court of Human Rights, notes that in Professor Rhys Jenkins's (University of East Anglia, School of Development Studies) work, he found that 41.6% of company codes contained clauses that there should be no forced labour, and 46.5% contained clauses that there should be no child labour, while only 23.8% mentioned freedom of association and collective bargaining.[42]

> In contrast to such internal monitoring, the credibility of the monitoring exercise and hence the legitimacy of the code will be heightened by external mechanisms. External monitoring involves the on-site inspection by a third-party, i.e. an external auditing firm hired by the corporation, to which the auditor reports.[43]

Also, even if the code itself is weak or less stringent, there is room for a very competent enforcement mechanism. "A survey of 132 codes by Kolk, for instance, found that 41% of the codes did not specifically mention monitoring and that where monitoring systems indeed had been in place, in 44% they relied on internal monitoring."[44] Keller notes that the WRC was founded by the United Students Against Sweatshops in 2000. The factory inspections are conducted by the WRC itself, and reports are posted on the WRC website.[45] This differs from the work of the FLA, which does not independently inspect factories. Also, the FLA is seen as more aligned with corporate interests.

Smyth et al. discuss the increase in suicides in Shenzhen, China's Foxconn factories in January–May 2010. "A report by the workers' rights watchdog, Solidarity International, suggests that a primary reason for the suicides is the adverse effects of excessive working hours."[46] Certain parts of the world have higher rates of overtime work which in some cases may be termed excessive hours. "According to the ILO (2006), in Thailand, 46.7 per cent of people work in excess of 48

Chains" *British Journal of Industrial Relations* vol 51 no 3 (Sep. 2013) pp. 519–552 at 524.

42 Helen Keller, "Corporate Codes of Conduct and Their Implementation: The Question of Legitimacy" University of Zurich Website, at 21.

43 Helen Keller, "Corporate Codes of Conduct and Their Implementation: The Question of Legitimacy" University of Zurich Website, at 22.

44 Helen Keller, "Corporate Codes of Conduct and Their Implementation: The Question of Legitimacy" University of Zurich Website, at 23.

45 Helen Keller, "Corporate Codes of Conduct and Their Implementation: The Question of Legitimacy" University of Zurich Website, at 53.

46 Russell Smyth et al., "Working Hours in Supply Chain Chinese and Thai Factories: Evidence from the Fair Labor Association's 'Soccer Project'" *British Journal of Industrial Relations* vol 51 no 2 (June 2013) pp. 382–408 at 383.

hours per week, which is the third highest in the world."[47] Smyth's study concludes that 48% of workers reported working in excess of 60 hours per week, which is the FLA code limit.[48] Often this is forced overtime, where workers do not have the ability to refuse such work. This may be more prevalent in workplaces where workers live onsite in dormitories, as the worker is less distanced from the workplace and more controlled by management.

Hsieh notes that it is argued that developed nations have a duty to those in developing nations. "The general idea of a duty to rescue has been articulated and discussed by a number of scholars as a plausible way to account for intuitions about a duty to provide aid to others."[49] This idea can be attributed to Peter Singer's work in 1972 about saving a drowning child if the only consequence to the rescuer is to muddy their clothes. "In turn, to the extent that members of developed economies can be considered to be in a state of emergency, citizens of developed economies are under a duty of rescue to provide assistance to members of developing economies (Ashford 2000)."[50] This is a better slant to take on the notion that developed nations should help developing nations – rather than have such help be interpreted as neo-colonialism or paternalism.

Lakhani, Kuruvilla, and Avgar note that "supplier firms in value chain configurations associated with low-skilled employees and low-employment stability will be less likely to invest in employment relations practices aimed at skill development and worker loyalty and more likely to adopt practices that minimize costs."[51] It is important to note that because much of the factory work done is unskilled or low skilled, the workers are easily replaced. There is less incentive for the company to keep on some workers over others, as opposed to workplaces where workers are highly skilled and more difficult to replace.

Oka notes that unions help reduce violations of labour standards, but "union presence affects certain dimensions of labour standards more than others. The regression analysis shows union presence is highly significant with regard to

47 Russell Smyth et al., "Working Hours in Supply Chain Chinese and Thai Factories: Evidence from the Fair Labor Association's 'Soccer Project'" *British Journal of Industrial Relations* vol 51 no 2 (June 2013) pp. 382–408 at 387.

48 Russell Smyth et al., "Working Hours in Supply Chain Chinese and Thai Factories: Evidence from the Fair Labor Association's 'Soccer Project'" *British Journal of Industrial Relations* vol 51 no 2 (June 2013) pp. 382–408 at 390.

49 Nien-he Hsieh, "Voluntary Codes of Conduct for Multinational Corporations: Coordinating Duties of Rescue and Justice" *Business Ethics Quarterly* vol 16 no 2 (2006) pp. 119–135 at 123.

50 Nien-he Hsieh, "Voluntary Codes of Conduct for Multinational Corporations: Coordinating Duties of Rescue and Justice" *Business Ethics Quarterly* vol 16 no 2 (2006) pp. 119–135 at 123.

51 Tashlin Lakhani, Sarosh Kuruvilla, & Ariel Avgar, "From the Firm to the Network: Global Value Chains and Employment Relations Theory" *British Journal of Industrial Relations* vol 51 no 3 (Sep. 2013) pp. 440–472 at 451.

wage, hours, and leave standards, but much less so vis-à-vis safety and health issues."[52]

Harry Arthurs notes that corporations superseding their reach through self-regulation is not new but is rather antiquated and a return to the old. He cites the examples of the Hudson's Bay Company and East India Tea Company as enormously powerful corporations that were almost state-like.[53] Rather than corporation-centred regulation being novel, it is in fact long-standing.

Weil and Mallo argue that there are three general mechanisms that address global labour standards: (1) a more traditional government role of monitoring codes or standards, (2) certification-based systems such as Social Accountability International (SAI) which has outside auditors, and (3) a mode that connects unions and organizations such as the Workers Rights Consortium (WRC) that is complaints-based.[54] The third model also makes use of the naming, shaming, and blaming approach to garner media attention about abusive labour practices to encourage consumers to boycott or buycott.[55]

Bondy, Matten, and Moon note that

> [s]elf-regulatory initiatives offer a means to control corporate behaviour across borders as they are not tied to any particular political system or territory, and therefore can be applied in a variety of locations within corporations, industries or sectors, depending on the scope of the initiative and the will of the corporation in implementation.[56]

The authors offer a definition of codes of conduct:

> CoCs can be defined as a voluntary set of commitments that either influence corporate attitudes and behaviours or are undertaken by the corporation to define their intentions and/or actions with regard to ethical and other issues, or towards a range of stakeholders from a market-based perspective.[57]

52 Chikako Oka, "Improving Working Conditions in Garment Supply Chains: The Role of Unions in Cambodia" *British Journal of Industrial Relations* (2015) pp. 1–26 at 20.

53 Harry W. Arthurs, "Private Ordering and Workers Rights in the Global Economy: Corporate Codes of Conduct as a Regime of Labour Market Regulation" (2002) Osgoode Digital Commons Paper 15, online: <http://digitalcommons.osgoode.yorku.ca/scholarly_works/15>, at 475.

54 David Weil & Carlos Mallo, "Regulating Labour Standards via Supply Chains: Combining Public/Private Interventions to Improve Workplace Compliance" *British Journal of Industrial Relations* vol 45 no 4 (Dec. 2007) pp. 791–814 at 793.

55 See note on page X about activists and targets.

56 Krista Bondy, Dirk Matten, & Jeremy Moon, "Codes of Conduct as a Tool for Sustainable Governance in MNCs" in S. Benn & D. Dunphy (eds.), *Corporate Governance and Sustainability: Challenges for Theory and Practice* (London: Routledge, 2006), at 6.

57 Krista Bondy, Dirk Matten, & Jeremy Moon, "Codes of Conduct as a Tool for Sustainable Governance in MNCs" in S. Benn & D. Dunphy (eds.), *Corporate Governance and Sustainability: Challenges for Theory and Practice* (London: Routledge, 2006), at 7.

The Clean Clothes Campaign outlines four major faults in codes of conduct: (1) they are vaguely defined, (2) they are incomplete – may exclude the right to organize, (3) not implemented – may lack information about how the codes are employed or monitored, and (4) not independently monitored – an internal monitoring system may not be sufficient.[58]

Williams, Davies, and Chinguno write about International Framework Agreements (IFAs) as a potential route to advance the rights of workers.[59] They note that IFAs are formed between MNCs and "global union federations." The authors note that approximately 80 agreements have been enacted.[60] While the authors are sceptical about how useful IFAs may be, they note that "IFAs have been seen as a step towards the internationalization of collective bargaining . . . By framing labour rights as universal human rights, IFAs can be seen as a form of 'stateless' regulation."[61] IFAs do seem to be more centred on local unions rather than codes of conduct which may be seen as being distant.

> Rather than attempting to "ratchet up" standards from afar, IFAs hold out the possibility of building sustainable local union capacity. It is this aim alone that avoids the charge made of voluntary corporate arrangements, that by casting workers as victims, rather than active agents, they risk further disempowering labour (Seidman 2007)."[62]

How are codes implemented?

How does a code of conduct get implemented? What mechanisms should be in place to ensure compliance and that the code will be well enforced?

Mamic goes into detail about each section that should be included in a code of conduct, from forced labour and child labour to freedom of association and

58 Krista Bondy, Dirk Matten, & Jeremy Moon, "Codes of Conduct as a Tool for Sustainable Governance in MNCs" in S. Benn & D. Dunphy (eds.), *Corporate Governance and Sustainability: Challenges for Theory and Practice* (London: Routledge, 2006), at 9.

59 I must note that I am sceptical about the promise of IFAs, as I first heard about them in the summer of 2011 from a Senior Partner at a management-side labour and employment law firm. If management-side law firms see them as beneficial, then maybe they are not very advantageous for workers.

60 Glynne Williams, Steve Davies, & Crispen Chinguno, "Subcontracting and Labour Standards: Reassessing the Potential of International Framework Agreements" *British Journal of Industrial Relations* vol 53 no 2 (June 2015) pp. 181–203 at 184.

61 Glynne Williams, Steve Davies, & Crispen Chinguno, "Subcontracting and Labour Standards: Reassessing the Potential of International Framework Agreements" *British Journal of Industrial Relations* vol 53 no 2 (June 2015) pp. 181–203 at 185.

62 Glynne Williams, Steve Davies, & Crispen Chinguno, "Subcontracting and Labour Standards: Reassessing the Potential of International Framework Agreements" *British Journal of Industrial Relations* vol 53 no 2 (June 2015) pp. 181–203 at 198.

Table 2.2 What does "minimum wage" mean?

Living wage	A wage that meets basic requirements related to food, health, social, leisure, and familial needs and obligations
Prevailing wage	The average rate paid to workers in a particular sector, which is often higher than the minimum wage given that specialized skills may be required
Fair wage	Similar in intent to "living wage," developed in response to what is perceived as unrealistically low minimum wage levels and taking into consideration the realities of daily life

Source: Ivanka Mamic, *Implementing Codes of Conduct: How Business Manage Social Performance in Global Supply Chains* (Geneva: Greenleaf Publishing, 2004), at 52–53.

collective bargaining. She notes that it is important to use precise language when drafting codes, such as not just listing that there should be no "forced labour" but also including what constitutes forced labour from prison work to bonded labour.[63] In regard to freedom of association, Mamic notes that corporations should avoid simply stating that the company agrees that workers should have the right to join a union, but also such additions as there will be no punishment or penalties for workers involved with union activity.[64] "Such rights, being more conceptual, are more likely to be expressed as a prohibition from interfering or restricting workers from pursuing means of collective representation."[65]

Mamic notes that the difference in language used among different codes is important.

Mamic notes that in the supply chain network there are many different entities. For example:

> Raw materials vendors → Tier II suppliers → Tier I suppliers → **MNE** → Distribution Centres → Retailers → Customer Zones[66]

This complex system means that it is more difficult to track a product from its inception to its final point of sale. However, it is not impossible. If a code is in place that includes each step in the process, then the process can be more regulated – similar to the Kimberly Process Certification System (KPCS). KPCS

63 Ivanka Mamic, *Implementing Codes of Conduct: How Business Manage Social Performance in Global Supply Chains* (Geneva: Greenleaf Publishing, 2004), at 49.

64 Ivanka Mamic, *Implementing Codes of Conduct: How Business Manage Social Performance in Global Supply Chains* (Geneva: Greenleaf Publishing, 2004), at 49.

65 Ivanka Mamic, *Implementing Codes of Conduct: How Business Manage Social Performance in Global Supply Chains* (Geneva: Greenleaf Publishing, 2004), at 50.

66 Adapted from Ivanka Mamic, *Implementing Codes of Conduct: How Business Manage Social Performance in Global Supply Chains* (Geneva: Greenleaf Publishing, 2004), at 68.

Table 2.3 Cost structure of the apparel industry

Cost components	*Percentage*
Retail shop profits and other costs (personnel, rent, administration, and advertising)	50
Brand profit, overhead, and promotion	25
Material costs and factory profits	13
Transportation/taxes/import costs	11
Factory workers' wages	1
Retail price	100

Source: Ivanka Mamic, *Implementing Codes of Conduct: How Business Manage Social Performance in Global Supply Chains* (Geneva: Greenleaf Publishing, 2004), at 154.

starts from the mining of the diamond onwards, so codes for apparel could include products from sourcing to manufacturing and retail.

If the cost of wages is examined when compared to the entire cost of making a product, it becomes obvious how low the wages are. This demonstrates that wages can be increased without causing too much detriment. Increasing wages is part of the solution, along with better working conditions, etc.

Codes – Corporation A, Corporation B, and Corporation C

I had gathered codes of conduct from 2012 as part of my earlier research into shareholder proposals. I chose the 2012 versions of the Corporation A, Corporation B, and Corporation C codes of conduct to examine in depth. I also tracked down how Corporation B and Corporation C codes have advanced since 2012. I chose to focus on these three codes, as they are all well-known companies and all in the apparel industry, so I am comparing companies that are similar rather than choosing an outlier. Corporation A was once a target by anti-sweatshop activists, and it is interesting to see how they have responded to such attention.

Corporation A

The Corporation A code from 2012 has not changed[67] since 2007. The code claims to be based on ILO core conventions and the Universal Declaration of Human Rights.[68] Part I outlines that Corporation A will comply with the law. Part II shows that Corporation A is committed to limiting its environmental impacts. Part III details labour provisions which include a ban on child labour,

67 The Corporation A Code was accessed in April 2016 and it is identical to the one located in 2012. The copyright on the code itself is 2007.

68 Corporation A Code of Vendor Conduct, 2007.

and discrimination as well as a ban on forced labor. The code also recognizes that workers are free to join unions and have a right to bargain collectively.[69] The code also states that "[a]s a condition of doing business with Corporation A, each and every factory must comply with this Code of Vendor Conduct. Corporation A will continue to develop monitoring systems to assess and ensure compliance."[70]

Corporation B

The Corporation B Code of Conduct for Suppliers in 2012[71] has been updated to include more information on freedom of association/collective bargaining, wages and benefits, working hours, and access to facilities which were absent from the earlier version. The section on access to facilities outlines that representatives of Corporation B should be allowed unrestricted access to suppliers' factories to ensure compliance with the code. These improvements have created a more fulsome code.

Corporation C

Corporation C's code in 2012 was quite extensive and included a "Whistle Blowing" hotline where complaints about violations of the code could be made Monday to Friday, 9 a.m. to 4 p.m. There was no mention of external monitoring, unlike the Corporation B code which has a monitoring program in the 2012 and 2016 versions (although the level of monitoring is not mentioned in the code). The Corporation C code does mention that "suppliers must participate in the Company's social compliance program, which may include but is not limited to disclosure of factories, participation in factory audits."[72] In the 2015 Corporation C, some sections from been moved from the 2012 version, but the code remains much the same.

The Corporation C code is the most stringent, as it also has a monitoring program, which is internal, to enforce the code. The elements are quite similar among the three codes, as they contain elements that are common in collective agreements which outline the workplace conditions, hours of work, etc. Even if the headings are similar, the level of detail in the Corporation A code and the Corporation B code is lower than that in the Corporation C code. Codes can cover many topics, but that also may be done in a shallow manner rather than having details that allow for greater uniformity. When the code lacks specificity, the code may be more open to being misinterpreted. When the code

69 Corporation A Code of Vendor Conduct, 2007.

70 Corporation A Code of Vendor Conduct, 2007.

71 I located this code in 2012, but there was no date on the document to ascertain when it was created.

72 Corporation C 2015.

Table 2.4 Comparison of the three codes

	Corporation A	*Corporation B 2016*	*Corporation C 2015*
Child labour	Yes	Yes	Yes
Forced labour	Yes	Yes	Yes
Wages and benefits	Yes	Yes	Yes
Overtime	Yes		Yes
Working hours	Yes	Yes	Yes
Working conditions	Yes	Yes	
Health and safety	Yes		Yes
Harassment	Yes		Yes
Discrimination	Yes	Yes	Yes
Environment	Yes	Yes	Yes
Freedom of association	Yes	Yes	Yes
Monitoring	Yes	Yes	Social compliance program
Access to facilities		Yes	

is very detailed, it provides less room for misinterpretation and allows for increased standardization.

Increasing labour standards on a worldwide level

This type of private regulation is outside of the state-centred regulation model and instead attempts to build a standard that is not based on national borders. "[S]ome multinational corporations and non-governmental organizations have struck out on their own, agreeing voluntarily to adopt various codes of conduct and allowing outsiders to verify compliance with these codes. In some cases these efforts have yielded impressive gains."[73] Sabel, O'Rourke and Fung seem to imply that codes of conduct have some value in building the rights of workers. This RLS model that the authors devised does not set out a regulatory framework or a way of making the theory practical. This notion of an industry-wide standard is worth pursuing, as then one is comparing like with like rather than trying to transcribe norms from one industry to another.

73 Charles Sabel, Dara O'Rourke, & Archon Fung, "Ratcheting Labor Standards: Regulation for Continuous Improvement in the Global Workplace" online: <http://papers.ssrn.com/sol3/papers.cfm?abstract_id=253833>, at 1.

Model code of conduct

While I was one of three law students who drafted the Queen's Code of Conduct (see earlier in this chapter), I find that the provisions could be improved. I am suggesting a model code of conduct. I agree with Professor Jill Murray's argument that the ILO Conventions are aimed at nation states and may be better suited to remain that way because states have enforcement mechanisms that other entities (corporations) lack. Reference to the ILO Conventions can help situate a code of conduct in a broader discussion about workers' rights and can be useful in that regard – to demonstrate that this one particular code of conduct is part of something larger. Professor John Ruggie's work on how states and corporations have a responsibility to protect human rights can also be incorporated in codes with reference to his report. I have indicated by footnote when the language in my model code is borrowed from other codes.

What are the basic provisions which should be included in all codes? As indicated in the chart detailing the comparison of the three Codes of Corporation A, Corporation B 2016, and Corporation C 2015 there are some areas that should be covered in all codes (Table 2.4). Number 11 is an advanced right of freedom of association and collective bargaining. Number 12 and 13 are more about enforcement and compliance. There should be a preamble outlining the purpose of the Code. A preamble is used in all three codes, and they are sufficient. The following headings and topics should be included:

1. Forced Labour
2. Child Labour
3. Wages and Benefits
4. Overtime
5. Working Hours
6. Working Conditions
7. Health and Safety
8. Harassment
9. Discrimination
10. Environment
11. Freedom of Association, Collective Bargaining
12. Monitoring
13. Access to Facilities

Model code of conduct

Corporation X is committed to ensuring that all of its products are produced in an ethical manner, consistent with international labour standards, and all applicable laws and regulations. This code provides the basic standard for Corporation X and all suppliers and sub-suppliers must comply with the provisions outlined in this code. Violations of this code may result in the termination of the contract between Corporation X and the supplier/subsupplier found to be in violation.

1. Forced labour

Employment must be voluntary, and respect the right of workers to decide to work or not. Suppliers must not use forced labour, whether in the form of prison labour, indentured labour, bonded labour, or otherwise. Slavery and human trafficking are prohibited.[74] Workers must have the right to refuse unsafe work.

2. Child labour

No person shall be employed at an age younger than 15 (or 14 where, consistent with International Labor Organization practices for developing countries under ILO Convention 138, the law of the country of manufacture allows such exception). Where the age for completing compulsory education is higher than the standard for the minimum age of employment stated above, the higher age for completing compulsory education shall apply to this section. Suppliers and sub-suppliers agree to work with governmental, human rights, and non-governmental organizations, as determined by the Corporation and supplier, to minimize the negative impact on any child released from employment as a result of the enforcement of this code.

Consistent with ILO Conventions 138 and 182, the minimum age for admission to any type of employment or work which by its nature or the circumstances in which it is carried out is likely to jeopardize the health, safety, or morals of young persons shall not be less than 18 years of age.[75]

While not a requirement, it would be beneficial if employers encouraged children to attend school/classes.

3. Wages and benefits

Suppliers and their contractors provide wages and benefits in the relevant industry, which constitutes a dignified living wage which is capable of providing for the essential needs of workers and their families.

A living wage shall be defined as a wage which provides for the basic needs (housing, energy, nutrition, clothing, health care, education, potable water, child care, transportation, and savings)[76] of an average family unit of employees in the relevant sector of the country divided by the average number of adult wage earners in the family unit of employees, in the relevant employment sector of the country.[77]

74 From Corporation C Code 2015.
75 From the Queen's Code.
76 This is similar to the definition of "living wage" offered by Mamic in Chapter 1 (page XX).
77 From the Queen's Code.

4. Overtime

In addition to their compensation for regular hours of work, employees shall be compensated for overtime hours at such a premium rate as is legally required in that country, or as negotiated in a collective agreement, but not less than at a rate equal to their regular hourly compensation rate.[78] Typical overtime rates are 1.5 times regular hourly rates. Also common is twice the hourly rate for workers working on statutory holidays.

5. Working hours

Except in extraordinary circumstances, employees shall (1) not be required to work more than the lesser of (a) 48 hours per week and 12 hours overtime per week, or (b) the limits on regular and overtime hours allowed by the law of the country of manufacture; and (2) be entitled to at least one day off in every seven-day period as well as holidays and vacations.[79]

6. Working conditions

Suppliers and their subcontractors are expected to treat all workers with respect and dignity and provide them with a safe and healthy work environment. Workers must not be subjected to corporal punishment or any other form of physical, psychological, sexual, or verbal harassment or abuse.

Supplier's factories must comply with all applicable laws and regulations relating to working conditions, including workers' health and safety. Factories must:

- Have adequate lighting in all areas.
- Be well ventilated. Windows, fans, air conditioners or heaters must be present where required in all work areas.
- Have sufficient, clearly marked, accessible exits allowing for orderly worker evacuation in case of any emergency.
- Have adequate fire alarm systems. Fire extinguishers must be appropriate to the types of possible fires in the various areas of the factory, be regularly maintained and charged, the date of last inspection must be displayed, and they must be mounted so they are visible and accessible in all areas.
- Conduct evacuation drills at least once per annum.
- Ensure that machinery is properly equipped with operational safety devices and inspected and serviced on a regular basis.

78 From the Queen's Code. The Queen's Code is the only one that includes overtime as a separate heading. The other codes that include the word only include it with working hours.

79 From the Queen's Code. The Queen's Code is the most detailed as other codes state things like the company must adhere to the law.

- Provide and allow workers reasonable access to drinkable water throughout the working day.
- Have a minimum of one well-stocked first aid kit and one or more employees trained in basic first aid. A procedure must be in place for handling injuries that require further medical evaluation and/or hospitalization. While not required, it would be useful to have one staff member who is trained in CPR.
- Maintain clean and sanitary toilet areas that are available to employees throughout their entire workday. There must be no unreasonable restrictions on their use.
- Store any hazardous and combustible materials which may be located on its premises in secure, ventilated areas. All safety and legal requirements must be met when disposing of such materials.
- In the event that dormitory facilities are provided for workers, ensure that those facilities meet all applicable laws and regulations related to wage deductions, health, safety and protection of employees, including fire, electrical, mechanical and structural safety, and sanitation.[80]

7. Health and safety

Suppliers must provide a safe and healthy work environment in a building that is structurally sound.[81] Suppliers must have a valid building and, where applicable, a construction license/certificate for the premises as required by local laws. Factories must provide adequate ventilation, first aid supplies, fire exits and safety equipment, well-lit workstations, clean washing facilities and an adequate number of toilets for both men and women, and access to clean drinking water; and suppliers must ensure that all are well maintained and in good working order as required by local laws. Factories must also have an adequate number of clearly marked, unlocked exits that are kept clear of any obstructions, and conduct a minimum of one emergency evacuation drill per year. Worker housing and dining facilities, where provided by supplier, must meet a reasonable standard of health and safety, and be separated from warehouse and production areas.[82]

8. Harassment

Every worker must be treated with respect and dignity. No worker may be subject to any physical, sexual, psychological, or verbal harassment or abuse,

80 Corporation B 2016.
81 This is especially important in light of Rana Plaza.
82 From Corporation C Code 2015.

including the use of physical punishment.[83] Employers are encouraged to create a collegial working environment.

9. Discrimination

Workers must not be subject to discrimination in employment, including with respect to hiring, salary, benefits, advancement, discipline, termination or retirement, on the basis of gender, race, religious or personal beliefs, age (other than normal and legally allowed hiring or retirement limitations), disability, sexual orientation, maternity or marital status, nationality, political opinion, union participation, social or ethnic origin or membership in any legal organization. Employment decisions must be made solely on the basis of knowledge, skill, efficiency, and ability to do the job and meet its requirements.[84]

10. Environment

The company will support suppliers who conduct their business using progressive environmental practices and take active steps to preserve and protect the well-being of the environment, including complying with all applicable laws and regulations in respect to protecting the environment and maintaining procedures for notifying local authorities in the event of an environmental accident resulting from supplier's operations.[85] Employers are encouraged to become knowledgeable about eco-friendly practices.

11. Freedom of association

Licensees and their contractors shall recognize and respect the right of employees to freedom of association and collective bargaining with bargaining representatives of their own choice. No employee shall be subject to harassment, intimidation, or retaliation as a result of his or her efforts to freely associate or bargain collectively. Where not explicitly prohibited by national laws, University licensees and contractors shall ensure compliance with ILO Conventions 87, 98, and 135.[86]

12. Monitoring

Where applicable, suppliers must participate in the company's social compliance program, which may include but is not limited to disclosure of factories, participation in factory audits, and inspection of books and records. If a supplier

83 From Corporation C Code 2015.
84 From Corporation C Code 2015.
85 From Corporation C Code 2015.
86 From the Queen's Code.

manages and enforces its own social compliance program, it must meet or exceed the compliance standards set forth in the company's program, and may be required to submit supporting documents to demonstrate same.[87]

13. Access to facilities

Suppliers must allow authorized representatives of Corporation X unrestricted access to their facilities and to all relevant records at all times, whether or not notified in advance, to ensure compliance with this code.[88]

Bibliography for Chapter 2

Legislation

Canada *Business Corporations Act*, RSC 1985, c C-44.

Caselaw

Macaura v Northern Assurance Co Ltd., 1925, AC 619.
Salomon *v Salomon & Co Ltd.*, 1897, AC 22.

Secondary sources

Books

Crane, Andrew, Dirk Matten, & Jeremy Moon, *Corporations and Citizenship* (Cambridge: Cambridge University Press, 2008).

Locke, Richard M., *The Promise and Limits of Private Power: Promoting Labor Standards in a Global Economy* (New York: Cambridge University Press, 2013).

Mamic, Ivanka, *Implementing Codes of Conduct: How Business Manage Social Performance in Global Supply Chains* (Geneva: Greenleaf Publishing, 2004).

Sukdeo, Vanisha H., *Regulation and Inequality at Work: Isolation and Inequality beyond the Regulation of Labour* (New York: Routledge, 2018).

Book chapters

Bondy, Krista, Dirk Matten, & Jeremy Moon, "Codes of Conduct as a Tool for Sustainable Governance in MNCs" in S. Benn & D. Dunphy, eds., *Corporate Governance and Sustainability: Challenges for Theory and Practice* (London: Routledge, 2006).

87 From Corporation C Code 2015. HBC also has a social compliance manual which is 41 pages long.

88 Corporation B 2016.

Articles

Arthurs, Harry W., "Private Ordering and Workers Rights in the Global Economy: Corporate Codes of Conduct as a Regime of Labour Market Regulation" (2002) *Osgoode Digital Commons* Paper 15 online: <http://digitalcommons.osgoode.yorku.ca/scholarly_works/15>.

Carroll, Archie, "A Three-Dimensional Conceptual Model of Corporate Performance" *The Academy of Management Review* vol 4 no 4 (October 1979) pp. 497–505.

Dhir, Aaron A., "Realigning the Corporate Building Blocks: Shareholder Proposals as a Vehicle for Achieving Corporate Social and Human Rights Accountability" *ABLJ* vol 43 (2006) p 365.

Dodd, E. Merrick, "For Whom Are Corporate Managers Trustees?" *Harvard Law Review* vol 45 no 7 (May 1932) pp. 1145–1163.

Ertimur, Yonca, Fabrizio Ferri, & Stephen R. Stubben, "Board of Directors' Responsiveness to Shareholders: Evidence from Shareholder Proposals" online: <www.hbs.edu/research/pdf/08-048.pdf>.

Goodpaster, Kenneth E., "Business Ethics and Stakeholder Analysis" *Business Ethics Quarterly* vol 1 no 1 (January 1991) pp. 53–73.

Hsieh, Nien-he, "Voluntary Codes of Conduct for Multinational Corporations: Coordinating Duties of Rescue and Justice" *Business Ethics Quarterly* vol 16 no 2 (2006) pp. 119–135.

Lakhani, Tashlin, Sarosh Kuruvilla, & Ariel Avgar, "From the Firm to the Network: Global Value Chains and Employment Relations Theory" *British Journal of Industrial Relations* vol 51 no 3 (September 2013) pp. 440–472.

Locke, Richard M, Ben A. Rissing, & Timea Pal, "Complements or Substitutes? Private Codes, State Regulation and the Enforcement of Labour Standards in Global Supply Chains" *British Journal of Industrial Relations* vol 51 no 3 (September 2013) pp. 519–552.

Oka, Chikako, "Improving Working Conditions in Garment Supply Chains: The Role of Unions in Cambodia" *British Journal of Industrial Relations* (2015) pp. 1–26.

O'Reilly, Jane, "Is Negative Attention Better Than No Attention? The Comparative Effects of Ostracism and Harassment at Work", online: <http://pubsonline.informs.org/doi/abs/10.1287/orsc.2014.0900>.

Sabel, Charles, Dara O'Rourke, & Archon Fung, "Ratcheting Labor Standards: Regulation for Continuous Improvement in the Global Workplace", online: <http://papers.ssrn.com/sol3/papers.cfm?abstract_id=253833>.

Sarra, Janis, "The Corporation as Symphony: Are Shareholders First Violin or Second Fiddle?" *University of British Columbia Law Review* vol 36 (2003) pp. 403–442.

Smyth, Russell et al., "Working Hours in Supply Chain Chinese and Thai Factories: Evidence from the Fair Labor Association's 'Soccer Project'" *British Journal of Industrial Relations* vol 51 no 2 (June 2013) pp. 382–408.

Sukdeo, Vanisha H., "What Is the Benefit of a 'Benefit Corporation'?: Examining the Advantages and Detriment" *Banking and Finance Law Review* vol 31 no 1 (2015) pp. 89–111.

Waitzer, Edward & Douglas Sarro, "Fiduciary Society Unleashed: The Road Ahead for the Financial Sector" *The Business Lawyer* vol 69 (August 2014) p 1091.

Weil, David & Carlos Mallo, "Regulating Labour Standards via Supply Chains: Combining Public/Private Interventions to Improve Workplace Compliance" *British Journal of Industrial Relations* vol 45 no 4 (December 2007) pp. 791–814.

Williams, Glynne, Steve Davies, & Crispen Chinguno, "Subcontracting and Labour Standards: Reassessing the Potential of International Framework Agreements" *British Journal of Industrial Relations* vol 53 no 2 (June 2015) pp. 181–203.
Zumbansen, Peer & Simon Archer, "The BCE Decision: Reflections on the Firm as a Contractual Organization" (2008) *Comparative Research in Law & Political Economy*. Research Paper No 17/2008, online: <http://digitalcommons.osgoode.yorku.ca/clpe/191>.

Websites

Larry Cata Backer blog post on September 21, 2013, online: <http://lcbackerblog.blogspot.ca/2013/09/changing-corporate-behavior-through.html>.
Helen Keller, "Corporate Codes of Conduct and Their Implementation: The Question of Legitimacy" University of Zurich website: <www.yale.edu/macmillan/Helen_Keller_Paper.pdf>, at 21.

3 Changes to corporate governance

Another route besides implementing codes of conduct to help regulate corporations, as discussed in Chapter 2, is the approach used by B Lab and other such organizations in getting hard law enacted. The movement from soft law to hard law in regards to corporations becoming more socially responsible can be termed the hardening of CSR in that what was once merely voluntary can become mandatory. This development can be seen in the creation of Benefit Corporations, a corporate form which originated from the work of B Lab pushing for the establishment of Benefit Corporations to force corporations that claimed to be socially responsible to put substance behind those claims. In addition, fiduciary duties have been expanded for all corporations, not just those corporations who hold themselves out as socially responsible. It is important to hold all corporations to a standard that is consistent and fair rather than to expect a select group of good corporations to be leaders in regards to governance. These two actions of moving all corporations to become more socially responsible and having some corporations act as CSR leaders is able to happen at the same time. It is not an either–or situation. This chapter will examine the changes to corporate governance that happen beyond codes of conduct, which includes the expansion of fiduciary duties in legislation and caselaw such as *Peoples* and *BCE*.

Expansion of fiduciary duties

Fiduciary duties can be expanded through caselaw and through legislation. In this chapter I discuss the cases of *Peoples* and *BCE*, as well as the fiduciary duties outlined in the *CBCA*. I will also describe how Benefit Corporations would fit within the Canadian legal landscape. A Benefit Corporation (BC) is a new corporate form implemented in the United States of America (U.S.) that is intended to make corporations more socially responsible by outlining obligations beyond shareholder wealth maximization.

Summary of *Peoples*

The 2004 Supreme Court of Canada case of *Peoples Department Stores Inc (Trustee of) v Wise* dealt with issues involving section 122 of the *CBCA* about

Directors' duties during an insolvency. Wise Stores Inc. acquired Peoples Department Stores Inc. from Marks and Spencer Canada Inc. The three Wise brothers were majority shareholders, Officers, and Directors of Wise, and the only directors of Peoples. They devised an arrangement by which Peoples would make all purchases from North American suppliers, and Wise would make all purchases from all other suppliers. The new policy was implemented on February 1, 1994, but before the end of the year, both Wise and Peoples declared bankruptcy. Peoples's trustee filed a petition against the Wise brothers. The trustee claimed that they had breached their duties as directors under section 122 of the *CBCA* as they had favoured the interests of Wise over Peoples to the detriment of Peoples's creditors. The fiduciary duty under s. 122(1)(*a*) of the *CBCA* requires Directors and Officers to act in good faith and honestly *vis-à-vis* the corporation. Directors and Officers will not be held to be in breach of the duty of care under s. 122(1)(*b*) of the *CBCA* if they act prudently and on a reasonably informed basis. The decisions of Directors and Officers must be reasonable business decisions in light of all the circumstances, including the prevailing socio-economic conditions, about which they knew or ought to have known.

> The principal question raised by this appeal is whether directors of a corporation owe a fiduciary duty to the corporation's creditors comparable to the statutory duty owed to the corporation. For the reasons that follow, we conclude that directors owe a duty of care to creditors, but that duty does not rise to a fiduciary duty. We agree with the disposition of the Quebec Court of Appeal. The appeal is therefore dismissed.[1]

Summary of *BCE*

The 2008 Supreme Court of Canada case of *BCE Inc v 1976Debentureholders* was a challenge by a group of debentureholders (bondholders) to the acquisition of BCE by a group of purchasers led by the Ontario Teachers Pension Plan Board. The deal, by way of leveraged buyout, might have increased market price of the shares so that shareholders would benefit, but the bondholders would likely see a reduction in the market value of their bonds by 20%. All three offers contemplated the addition of new debt for which Bell Canada, a wholly owned subsidiary of BCE, would be liable. The Supreme Court rejected the challenge by the debentureholders, holding that the Board had taken into account their interests. The bondholders sought relief by way of the oppression remedy under section 241 of the *CBCA*.

> The Quebec Superior Court, *per* Silcoff J., approved the arrangement as fair under the *CBCA* and dismissed the claims for oppression. The Quebec Court of Appeal found that the arrangement had not been shown to be

1 *Peoples Department Stores Inc (Trustee of) v Wise* [2004] 3 SCR 461 at para 1.

> fair and held that it should not have been approved. Thus, it found it unnecessary to consider the oppression claim.[2]

Expanding on the decision in *Peoples*, the Court held that where there is conflict among stakeholders, Directors and Officers must treat each stakeholder group fairly.

> The debentureholders at trial opposed the arrangement on a number of grounds. First, the debentureholders sought relief under the oppression provision in s. 241 of the *CBCA*. Second, they opposed court approval of the arrangement, as required by s. 192 of the *CBCA*, alleging that the arrangement was not "fair and reasonable" because of the adverse effect on their economic interests.[3]

As stated by Professor Anthony VanDuzer of the University of Ottawa, Faculty of Law, the *BCE* decision "creates a new but incomplete regime for the responsibilities of corporate directors and officers."[4]

The *CBCA* and directors' duties

Directors' duties are outlined in section 122 of the *CBCA*. While these duties are statute-based there are also fiduciary duties at common law that need to be explored in regard to benefit corporations. Section 122 states:

122. 1 Every director and officer of a corporation in exercising their powers and discharging their duties shall

- *a* act honestly and in good faith with a view to the best interests of the corporation; and
- *b* exercise the care, diligence and skill that a reasonably prudent person would exercise in comparable circumstances.

Duty to comply

2 Every director and officer of a corporation shall comply with this Act, the regulations, articles, by-laws and any unanimous shareholder agreement.

2 *BCE Inc v 1976 Debentureholders* [2008] 3 SCR 560 at para 2.

3 *BCE Inc v 1976 Debentureholders* [2008] 3 SCR 560 at para 22.

4 J. Anthony VanDuzer, "*BCE v 1976 Debentureholders*: The Supreme Court's Hits and Misses in Its Most Important Corporate Law Decision since *Peoples*" *UBC Law Review* vol 43 no 1 (2010) pp. 205–258.

No exculpation

3 Subject to subsection 146(5), no provision in a contract, the articles, the by-laws or a resolution relieves a director or officer from the duty to act in accordance with this Act or the regulations or relieves them from liability for a breach thereof.[5]

The *CBCA* is part of the bigger Canadian legal landscape in regards to governance. The provincial statutes relating to corporations, securities regulation, and tax legislation, among others, play a vital role in the entire picture that comprises the governance of corporations.

After *Peoples* and *BCE*, it is said that the shareholder primacy model is no longer the model used in assessing the duties of Directors. Instead, Directors now operate under the duty towards the "best interests of the corporation." This duty forces Directors to consider interests beyond mere shareholder wealth maximization and instead makes them include other stakeholders when making decisions.

In *Peoples*, the Supreme Court of Canada expanded the duties of Directors with a caveat for corporations that are facing bankruptcy. Cases have to be determined based on their facts, and the facts in *Peoples* do not necessarily alter the duties of Directors in solvent corporations.

> This case came before our Court on the issue of whether directors owe a duty to creditors. The creditors did not bring a derivative action or an oppression remedy application under the *CBCA*. Instead, the trustee, representing the interests of the creditors, sued the directors for an alleged breach of the duties imposed by s. 122(1) of the *CBCA*.[6]

The Court interpreted the duties under s. 122 as being in fact two separate duties.

> The first duty has been referred to in this case as the "fiduciary duty." It is better described as the "duty of loyalty." We will use the expression "statutory fiduciary duty" for purposes of clarity when referring to the duty under the *CBCA*. This duty requires directors and officers to act honestly and in good faith with a view to the best interests of the corporation. The second duty is commonly referred to as the "duty of care." Generally speaking, it imposes a legal obligation upon directors and officers to be diligent in supervising and managing the corporation's affairs.[7]

5 *Canada Business Corporations Act*, RSC 1985, c C-44 at s 122.
6 *Peoples Department Stores Inc (Trustee of) v Wise* [2004] 3 SCR 461 at para 30.
7 *Peoples Department Stores Inc (Trustee of) v Wise* [2004] 3 SCR 461 at para 32.

While the Court has somewhat altered the duty, it is still reluctant to expand the duty too widely.

> This appeal does not relate to the non-statutory duty directors owe to shareholders. It is concerned only with the statutory duties owed under the *CBCA*. Insofar as the statutory fiduciary duty is concerned, it is clear that the phrase the "best interests of the corporation" should be read not simply as the "best interests of the shareholders."[8]

What is the extent of the duty? And to whom is it owed?

> We accept as an accurate statement of law that in determining whether they are acting with a view to the best interests of the corporation, it may be legitimate, given all the circumstances of a given case, for the board of directors to consider, *inter alia*, the interests of shareholders, employees, suppliers, creditors, consumers, governments and the environment.[9]

In *BCE*, the Supreme Court of Canada again altered the duty of Directors but so slightly that how these effects change on the ground is still being discussed by academics and practitioners. The Court outlined that shareholders are not the only concern for Directors. This context of pitting shareholders against bondholders is rather limited in that the true conflict is between those who have an actual contract with the corporation, the bondholders, and the shareholders.

> A share "is not an isolated piece of property . . . [but] a 'bundle' of interrelated rights and liabilities": *Sparling v. Quebec (Caisse de dépôt et placement du Québec)*, [1988] 2 S.C.R. 1015, at p. 1025, *per* La Forest J. These rights include the right to a proportionate part of the assets of the corporation upon winding-up and the right to oversee the management of the corporation by its board of directors by way of votes at shareholder meetings.[10]

However, if Directors are in what appears to be a conflict between whose rights take priority, the duty is to the corporation itself, not to the shareholders.

> The fiduciary duty of the directors to the corporation originated in the common law. It is a duty to act in the best interests of the corporation. Often the interests of shareholders and stakeholders are co-extensive with

8 *Peoples Department Stores Inc (Trustee of) v Wise* [2004] 3 SCR 461 at para 42.
9 *Peoples Department Stores Inc (Trustee of) v Wise* [2004] 3 SCR 461 at para 42.
10 *BCE Inc v 1976 Debentureholders* [2008] 3 SCR 560 at para 35.

> the interests of the corporation. But if they conflict, the directors' duty is clear – it is to the corporation: *Peoples Department Stores.*[11]

In paragraph 40 of the decision, the Court is borrowing the language from paragraph 42 of *Peoples.*

> In considering what is in the best interests of the corporation, directors may look to the interests of, *inter alia*, shareholders, employees, creditors, consumers, governments and the environment to inform their decisions. Courts should give appropriate deference to the business judgment of directors who take into account these ancillary interests, as reflected by the business judgment rule.[12]

The Court also introduces this concept of "fairness" into its analysis of *BCE.*

> Directors or other corporate actors may make corporate decisions or seek to resolve conflicts in a way that abusively or unfairly maximizes a particular group's interest at the expense of other stakeholders. The corporation and shareholders are entitled to maximize profit and share value, to be sure, but not by treating individual stakeholders unfairly.[13]

The Court also introduces this notion of a corporation as a "good corporate citizen." "The Court provides no substance or context for the assertions that both the directors and the corporation itself have a duty of 'good corporate citizenship.'"[14] Is the Court unilaterally imposing CSR standards on to corporations?

> Directors, acting in the best interests of the corporation, may be obliged to consider the impact of their decisions on corporate stakeholders, such as the debentureholders in these appeals. This is what we mean when we speak of a director being required to act in the best interests of the corporation viewed as a good corporate citizen. However, the directors owe a fiduciary duty to the corporation, and only to the corporation.[15]

The Court's distinction of whether the Directors owe a duty to shareholders or to the corporation itself is rather hollow, as the corporation itself encompasses shareholders plus other stakeholders. A duty to just the corporation is rather

11 *BCE Inc v 1976 Debentureholders* [2008] 3 SCR 560 at para 37.
12 *BCE Inc v 1976 Debentureholders* [2008] 3 SCR 560 at para 40.
13 *BCE Inc v 1976 Debentureholders* [2008] 3 SCR 560 at para 64.
14 Sarah P. Bradley, "BCE Inc. v. 1976 Debenture-Holders: The New Fiduciary Duties of Fair Treatment, Statutory Compliance and Good Corporate Citizenship?" *Ottawa Law Review* vol 41 (2009–2010) pp. 325–349 at para 42.
15 *BCE Inc v 1976 Debentureholders* [2008] 3 SCR 560 at para 66.

meaningless, as the corporation is a separate legal entity which contains no people, etc., and having a duty to such an entity must mean that others are owed the duty instead.

> In such cases, it is important to be clear that the directors owe their duty to the corporation, not to stakeholders, and that the reasonable expectation of stakeholders is simply that the directors act in the best interests of the corporation.[16]

In *BCE*, the Court is in fact revisiting the stakeholder debates from the 1930s. This is evidenced in paragraph 81 of the decision.

> As discussed, conflicts may arise between the interests of corporate stakeholders *inter se* and between stakeholders and the corporation. Where the conflict involves the interests of the corporation, it falls to the directors of the corporation to resolve them in accordance with their fiduciary duty to act in the best interests of the corporation, viewed as a good corporate citizen.[17]

Dodd wrote that Directors have a sole responsibility to shareholders. "The directors and other agents are fiduciaries carrying on the business in the sole interest of the stockholders."[18] This is far removed from the argument that stakeholders have interests in the corporation. Recall Berle's argument that Directors have a duty to others beyond shareholders.[19]

> Now I submit that you can not abandon emphasis on "the view that business corporations exist for the sole purpose of making profits for their stockholders" until such time as you are prepared to offer a clear and reasonably enforceable scheme of responsibilities to someone else.[20]

More current literature, such as Baron, notes that not all actions that can be termed to be socially responsible are for the good of the public. "That is, if the motivation is to serve society, at the cost of profits, the action is socially

16 *BCE Inc v 1976 Debentureholders* [2008] 3 SCR 560 at para 66.

17 *BCE Inc v 1976 Debentureholders* [2008] 3 SCR 560 at para 81.

18 E. Merrick Dodd, "For Whom Are Corporate Managers Trustees?" *Harvard Law Review* vol 45 no 7 (May 1932) pp. 1145–1163 at 1146.

19 "Most students of corporation finance dream of a time when corporate administration will be held to a high degree of required responsibility-a responsibility conceived not merely in terms of stockholders' rights, but in terms of economic government satisfying the respective needs of investors, workers, customers, and the aggregated community."

Adolf A. Berle, "For Whom Corporate Managers Are Trustees: A Note" *Harvard Law Review* vol 45 no 8 (June 1932) pp. 1365–1372 at 1372.

20 Adolf A. Berle, "For Whom Corporate Managers Are Trustees: A Note" *Harvard Law Review* vol 45 no 8 (June 1932) pp. 1365–1372 at 1367.

responsible, but if the motivation is to serve the bottom line, then the action is privately responsible."[21]

As noted by Dhir, "[t]he corollary of permitting directors to consider non-shareholder interests in fulfilling their duties to the corporation is that their doing so will not result in a violation of their fiduciary duty."[22] Dhir's argument is that considering stakeholder interests beyond shareholders is not a breach of the fiduciary duty. However, the counterargument of not being able to serve two masters is still apt. "[A] manager told to serve two masters (a little for the equity holders, a little for the community) has been freed of both and is answerable to neither."[23] The main thrust of the arguments that BCs force Directors into difficult positions about fiduciary duties can be summarized by the lack of expertise that some Directors may have in this arena. "Do directors themselves have the necessary tools and knowledge base to actually engage in a meaningful assessment of non-shareholder interests? If they do not, how can this be remedied?"[24]

New corporate forms of organization – Benefit Corporations

I will explore the new corporate form of BCs and how they would fit into the Canadian legal landscape by examining the *Canada Business Corporations Act ("CBCA")*,[25] *BCE Inc v 1976Debentureholders* (*BCE*),[26] and *Peoples Department Stores Inc (Trustees of) v Wise* (*Peoples*).[27] I will then turn to fiduciary duties at common law and the stakeholder debates will be explored to examine how much involvement and consideration is due to those beyond shareholders. I will look to British Columbia (B.C.) in regards to its Bill 23 which would enact a new corporate form of the Community Contribution Company (CCC) and the United Kingdom (U.K.) briefly for its use of the Community Interest Company (CIC) legislation. My conclusion will demonstrate that while BCs seem like a useful tool in the fight towards making corporations more socially responsible, they may prove ineffective if the Directors' duties are not clearly

21 Abigail McWilliams, Donald S. Siegel, & Patrick M. Wright, "Corporate Social Responsibility: Strategic Implications" *Journal of Management Studies* vol 43 no 1 (Jan. 2006) pp. 0022–2380 at 9.

22 Aaron Dhir, "The Politics of Knowledge Dissemination: Corporate Reporting, Shareholder Voice, and Human Rights" *Osgoode Hall LJ* vol 47 (2009) pp. 47–83 at 79.

23 Quoting Frank H. Easterbrook & Daniel R. Fischel, in Aaron Dhir, "The Politics of Knowledge Dissemination: Corporate Reporting, Shareholder Voice, and Human Rights" *Osgoode Hall LJ* vol 47 (2009) pp. 47–83 at 80.

24 Aaron Dhir, "The Politics of Knowledge Dissemination: Corporate Reporting, Shareholder Voice, and Human Rights" *Osgoode Hall LJ* vol 47 (2009) pp. 47–83 at 80.

25 *Canada Business Corporations Act*, RSC 1985, c C-44.

26 *BCE Inc v 1976 Debentureholders* [2008] 3 SCR 560.

27 *Peoples Department Stores Inc (Trustee of) v Wise* [2004] 3 SCR 461.

outlined and defined. Benefit Corporations are discussed in more detail in some of my other research.[28]

Fiduciary duties[29]

Holding multiple fiduciary duties seems to be a paradox. However, in Europe there are multi-stakeholder agreements that demonstrate that this can be accomplished. Hopefully, future caselaw will help to set parameters on the duties of Directors of BCs. The Business Law Section of the State Bar of California asserted that the BC legislation in its state would alter fiduciary duties. "The Bill represents a fundamental shift away from the traditional fiduciary duty principles which require directors to act in the best interests of the corporations and its shareholders."[30] The Corporations Committee also put forward that legislation is not needed in order to affiliate with B Lab. "Even without passage of the Bill, California corporations will continue to be free to associate themselves with B Lab and the 'benefit corporation' movement it seeks to foster."[31] This misses the point, as the difference between hard law (legislation) and soft law (in this case a voluntary certification scheme) is not being given enough weight. The underlying concern that certain items are law and others are not is not addressed by the Corporations Committee. As noted by Bradley,

> [i]n this context, fiduciary duties are generally owed to the dependent person(s) whose reasonable expectations they are intended to protect, while the statutory fiduciary duty in corporate law is always owed to the corporation itself; the reasonable expectations of others are external to this relationship.[32]

While reasonable expectations may not occupy a paramount position in regards to corporate law, the nature of the mundane duties needs to be drawn out. Fiduciary duties arise in the law of trusts, within parent-child relationships, and are held to be the utmost duty of one towards another.

28 For more information about Benefit Corporations, please see Vanisha H. Sukdeo, "What Is the Benefit of a 'Benefit Corporation'? Examining the Advantages and Detriment" *Banking and Finance Law Review* vol 31 no 1 (2015) pp. 89–111.

29 Please see Chapter 1 for a more complete discussion of fiduciary duties.

30 The State Bar of California, Business Law Section, Memo to Jared Huffman, online: <www.thecorporatecounsel.net/nonMember/docs/04_26_11_AB361.pdf>, at 1.

31 The State Bar of California, Business Law Section, Memo to Jared Huffman, online: <www.thecorporatecounsel.net/nonMember/docs/04_26_11_AB361.pdf>, at 4.

32 Sarah P. Bradley, "BCE Inc. v. 1976 Debenture-Holders: The New Fiduciary Duties of Fair Treatment, Statutory Compliance and Good Corporate Citizenship?" *Ottawa Law Review* vol 41 (2009–2010) pp. 325–349 at para 23.

> The basic nominate function of directors is to manage or direct the business of the corporation. Fiduciary accountability attaches to every aspect of that function. Each power (more broadly, each aspect of limited access) is capable of being turned to personal ends.[33]

Professor Benjamin Richardson's work in socially responsible investment is significant for its research on fiduciary duties. According to Richardson, "the fiduciary's foremost duty is one of loyalty to the beneficiary – to act in their sole or best interests."[34]

The Directors' duties under the *CBCA* has already been discussed. However, the term "fiduciary duty" only appears 16 times in eight different federal statutes[35] (appearing twice in each of the eight statutes). This not a vast landscape for fiduciary duties as defined at the federal level. This movement from state-made law to judge-made law through legislation to the common law system is tantamount in Canadian law. Only once BC legislation has been tested in the courts will a true answer about fiduciary duties have an outcome in regard to the duality of the duties under BC legislation.

What comes after *Peoples* and *BCE*?

Peoples was decided in 2004, and *BCE* was decided only four years later in 2008. Corporate law should expect for another important case to advance fiduciary duties. As VanDuzen noted, *BCE* created new and *incomplete* duties. A new Supreme Court case in the realm of corporate law and Directors' duties would help to complete the progress that was made in *BCE* and build upon those developments. The move from the best interests of the corporation being read as the "best of shareholders" to the "best interests of the corporation as a whole" means that the Canadian legal landscape is moving towards a stakeholder model of corporate governance where all stakeholders have voice and recognition. While *Peoples* was set against a backdrop of insolvency and *BCE* was focused on bondholders as the main group rather than shareholders, perhaps the time has come for shareholders in a solvent company to have a leading case that decides about whose interests take priority in regards to making decisions. This may create an artificial ranking of priority groups, but if such a case existed, it

33 Robert Flannigan, "Fiduciary Duties of Shareholders and Directors" *JBL* (May 2004) pp. 277–302 at 283.

34 Benjamin J. Richardson, "Do the Fiduciary Duties of Pension Funds Hinder Socially Responsible Investment?" *BLFR* vol 22 no 2 (2007) pp. 145–201 at 150.

35 *Bank Act* SC 1991, c 46, s 106 and s 125, *Bankruptcy and Insolvency Act* RSC 1985, c B-3, s 13 and s 14, *CBCA*, s 61 and s 75, *Canada Cooperatives Act* SC 1998, c 1, s 214 and s 236, *Canada Not-for-Profit Corporations Act* SC 2009, c 23, s 71, *Cooperative Credit Associations Act* SC 1991, c 48, s 113 and s 132, *Insurance Companies Act* SC 199, c 47, s 110 and s 129, *Trust and Loan Companies Act* SC 1991, c 45, s 109 and s 128.

might help to clarify whose interests are of the utmost importance and whose interests simply need to be considered. Neither *Peoples* nor *BCE* creates such a ranking. While this approach may seem formulaic, it is worthy of discussion. Also, perhaps such a ranking could be enacted in the legislation and allow for greater clarity for directors and officers.

Ethical consumption

Ethical consumption is the theory that certain consumers make their purchasing choices based on how ethically sourced and produced the products are. Studies show that ethical consumers tend to be affluent and highly educated, which may show a link between making ethical choices and *being able to afford* to make ethical choices. Advocates even use social media to bring attention to companies that use non-Canadian products and try to create a boycott of products that stop using Canadian products.[36]

Myth of the ethical consumer

There is much debate about whether the ethical consumer actually exists. Even if that person does exist, they are likely a very small group with certain privileges – they are likely more affluent than the average consumer, and likely to be more educated.

> Despite the hype, the reality is that most "ethical" products have occupied niche market positions except in the few circumstances in which major multinational corporations have taken on the cause and marketed these products broadly and as replacements for conventional offerings, such as Unilever and Ben & Jerry's (Hays 2000; Austin and Quinn 2007) or Starbucks and Fairtrade coffee (argenti 2004).[37]

This may be different from the conception of a corporation that ensures that all of its products are fairly produced. In the case of Starbucks, it may be that some but not all of its products are fair – it is up to the consumer to choose which of Starbucks' products to purchase rather than choosing another corporation where all of the items are fairly produced. "Hence, if Starbucks or Caribou Coffee switch to more Fairtrade sourcing, this does not imply anything about consumer desires, because the corporation is making the choice and not the individual (other than the consumer not revolting at the action)."[38] This raises

36 See in mainstream media the stir about Heinz not using Ontario tomatoes to produce its ketchup, while rival French's uses Leamington tomatoes.

37 Timothy M. Divinney, Pat Auger, & Giana M. Eckhardt, *The Myth of the Ethical Consumer* (Cambridge: Cambridge University Press, 2010), at 3.

38 Timothy M. Divinney, Pat Auger, & Giana M. Eckhardt, *The Myth of the Ethical Consumer* (Cambridge: Cambridge University Press, 2010), at 3.

an interesting hypothetical where a consumer may rebel against ethical products. This may be for a variety of reasons, including increased costs typically associated with ethical products. "The ethical consumer is a myth in its form of a heroic but uniquely unattainable role model."[39] However, some consumers may choose certain products for ethical reasons and not be swayed when making other choices (brand loyalty, etc.). "In this sense, it is the moral standard that creates the guilt surrounding our typical self-interested behavior."[40] The notion of guilt and the creation of the ethical consumer is important. Whether those consumers who are better informed actually make choices based on that acquired knowledge is interesting.[41] "The question then becomes one of asking: 'How important is the ethical issue when compared to other basic issues?' This answer is critical in a world where trade-offs are not free and social agendas are in competition."[42]

The notion that consumers are pulled in various directions due to competing "ethical choices" is also important. Does a consumer choose the product that is eco-friendly and has not mentioned the treatment of workers? Or the product that claims to be "sweatshop free" but does not mention environmental impact? Does such a product exist that satisfies both, or are the two variables in competition? "In its broadest form, C_NSR [consumer social responsibility] can be defined as the conscious and deliberate choice to make certain consumption choices based on personal and moral beliefs."[43] But consumers may hold multiple beliefs in regards to their purchasing choices and how those choices are impacted.

> Since the governments are in the pockets of businesses, who's going to control this most powerful institution? Business is more powerful than politics, and it's more powerful than religion. So it's going to have to be the vigilante consumer. – Anita Roddick[44]

Roddick introduces the term "vigilante consumer," which I take to mean that the consumer can "right the wrong" on his/her own rather than waiting for the state to act.

39 Timothy M. Divinney, Pat Auger, & Giana M. Eckhardt, *The Myth of the Ethical Consumer* (Cambridge: Cambridge University Press, 2010), at 4.
40 Timothy M. Divinney, Pat Auger, & Giana M. Eckhardt, *The Myth of the Ethical Consumer* (Cambridge: Cambridge University Press, 2010), at 5.
41 I want to pursue this argument further in another piece, "More of Law and Psychology."
42 Timothy M. Divinney, Pat Auger, & Giana M. Eckhardt, *The Myth of the Ethical Consumer* (Cambridge: Cambridge University Press, 2010), at 9.
43 Timothy M. Divinney, Pat Auger, & Giana M. Eckhardt, *The Myth of the Ethical Consumer* (Cambridge: Cambridge University Press, 2010), at 9.
44 Timothy M. Divinney, Pat Auger, & Giana M. Eckhardt, *The Myth of the Ethical Consumer* (Cambridge: Cambridge University Press, 2010), at 16.

> However, I may not care about that aspect of the product at all, and so the signal, while existing, has no value to me. I may "look for the union label," but doing so says nothing about my opinion about the ethics of unions.[45]

While the label may not speak to one's thoughts about the ethics of unions, it does speak to the fact that one's purchasing choice is influenced by "the union label."

> So, too, ethical consumers believe that they are controllers of their behaviors, doing good by purchasing correctly. However, there is an Olympus of firms and markets that create the contexts in which behavior occurs, giving an illusion of free will that is only partially free, and free in ways that are obscure.[46]

While the ethical consumer may be exercising free will, this may be an illusion of freedom in that the products offered are not limitless.

International regulation

In her book on the ILO Conventions, Jill Murray posits that the Conventions are a form of governance.

> The rules of the ILO and the Community can be compared as examples of transnational labour regulation. Each rule of these bodies is the product of consideration of two fundamental questions: why should a rule be made at the international level, and if one is to be made, what form should it take vis-à-vis national regulatory norms and procedures?[47]

However, she stipulates that the ILO Conventions are not readily transferable to the realm of corporate governance. Corporations do not have the same availability of enforcement that is available to the state.

> It is argued here that it is both valid and useful to study the ILO Conventions in their own right, independently of their ratification and implementation at the national level. The Conventions can be studied as a body of

45 Quoted in Timothy M. Divinney, Pat Auger, & Giana M. Eckhardt, *The Myth of the Ethical Consumer* (Cambridge: Cambridge University Press, 2010), at 22.

46 Timothy M. Divinney, Pat Auger, & Giana M. Eckhardt, *The Myth of the Ethical Consumer* (Cambridge: Cambridge University Press, 2010), at 36.

47 Jill Murray, *Transnational Labour Regulation: The ILO and EC Compared* (Norwell: Kluwer Law International, 2001), at 4–5.

> rules which reflects the views of the tripartite delegates of the ILO Member States at the International Labour Conference in any given year.[48]

Because of the malleability of the Conventions, she argues that they are not quite as useful as thought.

> The character of transnational labour rules of the ILO and the Community is thus at times rather difficult to capture. For the most part, they are not instruments of direct "governance," and they do not "regulate" as national legislation does. The details in international rules are often templates for multiple outcomes within and between national jurisdictions.[49]

In Novitz and Mangan the authors state that

> First, it is evident that labour standards which secure access to material well-being, such as non-discrimination in access to jobs and provision of a living wage, can assist in addressing poverty, thereby raising levels of economic development. Second, regulation of working conditions, such as hours of work and health and safety, can enable workers not only to make economic provision for their families but to care for their dependents, thereby promoting social cohesion, well-being and stability.[50]

Murray notes that "we need to critically assess the use of ILO standards *by firms*. ILO conventions are *addressed to states*."[51] This may not be an easy task to force companies to act like states and have the same obligations that we expect states to have. "As George Barnes – one of the group which negotiated the creation of the ILO – noted, it was feared that 'capital has no country' (Barnes 1926: 36)."[52] Have a rule/law that moves with the corporation, such as a code. The code is in place no matter what jurisdiction the company is in.

As noted by Barrientos, "[t]racing the supply, or value chain allows us to situate employment within the context of global sourcing, and helps to

48 Jill Murray, *Transnational Labour Regulation: The ILO and EC Compared* (Norwell: Kluwer Law International, 2001), at 5.
49 Jill Murray, *Transnational Labour Regulation: The ILO and EC Compared* (Norwell: Kluwer Law International, 2001), at 7.
50 Tonia Novitz & David Mangan, eds., *The Role of Labour Standards in Development: From Theory to Sustainable Practice?* (New York: Oxford University Press, 2011), at 4–5.
51 Jill Murray, "Labour Rights/Corporate Responsibilities: The Role of ILO Labour Standards" in Rhys Jenkins, Ruth Pearson, & Gill Seyfang (eds.), *Corporate Responsibility and Labour Rights: Codes of Conduct in the Global Economy* (London: Earthscan Publications Limited, 2002), at 31 (emphasis in original).
52 Jill Murray, "Labour Rights/Corporate Responsibilities: The Role of ILO Labour Standards" in Rhys Jenkins, Ruth Pearson, & Gill Seyfang (eds.), *Corporate Responsibility and Labour Rights: Codes of Conduct in the Global Economy* (London: Earthscan Publications Limited, 2002), at 33.

understand the different factors affecting conditions of work (Barrientos, forthcoming)."[53] Work, like capital, is able to transcend borders, but in a different way. Workers are less likely to move to another jurisdiction, but the nature of work has changed. A single product can be sourced and then assembled in numerous jurisdictions, and then shipped to another country to be purchased. "The ultimate sanction against non-compliance is the threat of being de-listed as a supplier. Codes are thus only 'voluntary' to the suppliers in that the alternative is to find new outlets."[54] This is an important point, as the degree of voluntariness is subject to change and is different from company to company and from supplier to supplier.

> Yet there are others who are more optimistic, seeing codes as offering a potential tool in efforts to promote worker organization and education. However, this will only be possible if workers have a sense of ownership, if they feel that codes are actually there to support them.[55]

If workers are able to be involved with the drafting and implementation of the code, they may feel more connected to it.

Actual impact on the ground

How much impact will codes make on those workers who actually produce the goods? It seems as though some citizens in developed countries are fighting on behalf of those workers in developing nations, which seems paternalistic. Also, who is to say that these workers want this help? In some instances, working in a sweatshop is a step up from other possible jobs (picking through trash, etc.).

Jacqueline Novogratz raises questions about compassion more broadly and how this impacts how people view corporations and their role in society. "Cote d'Ivoire became a place where just walking down the street filled me with questions about justice and compassion, power and money, and the randomness of where we are born and how much that determines who we become."[56] This

53 Stephanie Barrientos, "Mapping Codes through the Value Chain: From Researcher to Detective" in Rhys Jenkins, Ruth Pearson, & Gill Seyfang (eds.), *Corporate Responsibility and Labour Rights: Codes of Conduct in the Global Economy* (London: Earthscan Publications Limited, 2002), at 64.

54 Stephanie Barrientos, "Mapping Codes through the Value Chain: From Researcher to Detective" in Rhys Jenkins, Ruth Pearson, & Gill Seyfang (eds.), *Corporate Responsibility and Labour Rights: Codes of Conduct in the Global Economy* (London: Earthscan Publications Limited, 2002), at 67.

55 Linda Shaw & Angela Hale, "The Emperor's New Clothes: What Codes Mean for Workers in the Garment Industry" in Rhys Jenkins, Ruth Pearson, & Gill Seyfang (eds.), *Corporate Responsibility and Labour Rights: Codes of Conduct in the Global Economy* (London: Earthscan Publications Limited, 2002), at 109.

56 Jacqueline Novogratz, *The Blue Sweater: Bridging the Gap between Rich and Poor in an Interconnected World* (New York: Rodale Books, 2009), at 20.

extends to a notion of valuing humans in other jurisdictions. If we choose to devalue the humanity of others – how much are we willing to do so? By 5%? By 50%? What is a "tolerable" amount compared to the West/North?

> At the Philanthropy Workshop, we studied Rockefeller, of course, and Andrew Carnegie, another American industrialist who believed that men of great wealth had a duty to contribute to social, cultural, and economic life and improve the world. He wrote that "the man who dies, leaving behind him millions of available wealth, which was free for him to administer during life, will pass away unwept, unhonored, and unsung."[57]

This notion of the rich having to play guardian to the poor has both negative and positive connotations. It can be interpreted to mean that the rich are better than the poor and have to take care of the poor, versus it could mean that the rich individuals in society should share their wealth with others to help society more broadly.

> Next we had to obtain approval from the IRS as a nonprofit organization, no easy task in 2001 given that there was no exact precedent for what we wanted to do. We were completely agnostic as to whether change came through non-profit or for-profit channels; in fact, we believed it would come through both and often in partnership. Thankfully, our lawyers were able to register Acumen Fund as a public charity on April 1, 2001.[58]

Codes of conduct versus IFAs

Codes of conduct are a soft law mechanism that may be used to create a voluntary standard or set of rules to which corporations are bound. While this may be viewed as rather inadequate compared to legislation, codes of conduct have value in terms of allowing the two (or more) parties that are bound by the code to have direct input in drafting the code. While the inherent imbalance of power involved in the dynamics of the employment relationship between management and workers must be acknowledged and must have an impact on the creation of the code, it does allow for involvement while legislation does not.

IFAs involve the input of unions in the drafting. This option seems limited, as this only applies to workers who have a union. IFAs may be beneficial to unionized workers, but codes of conduct are more far reaching as codes are also available to non-unionized workers.

57 Jacqueline Novogratz, *The Blue Sweater: Bridging the Gap between Rich and Poor in an Interconnected World* (New York: Rodale Books, 2009), at 127.

58 Jacqueline Novogratz, *The Blue Sweater: Bridging the Gap between Rich and Poor in an Interconnected World* (New York: Rodale Books, 2009), at 193.

Greenwashing, or failure to have actions that back up claims

The term "greenwashing" is used in the environmental realm to describe the incident of a corporation claiming to care about the environment and CSR while not actual doing anything to back up its claims. This may also be deemed "paying lip service" to CSR principles while not actually putting any new ideas into play. This allows a corporation to enjoy the benefits of being seen as socially responsible without having to actually do anything that results in energy or monetary expenditures.

Globalization and self-regulation

As Prakash Sethi argues, globalization has fueled self-regulation.

> A company-based code of conduct is the most likely initial corporate response to social pressures, especially when the issues involved emanate directly from the company's core business operations. A company-based code provides its sponsor considerable flexibility in defining the parameter of the social issue in contention-especially in its earlier stages of public awareness.[59]

Some codes are more detailed, while others are almost superficial in that they are too short. "Another perverse outcome of this approach is that it may lead the code effort to be captured by the companies with the least amount of commitment to code compliance. This situation is akin to the capture theory of regulation, where the regulators are co-opted by the regulated and thus lose their legitimacy as regulators (Thompson 2003)."[60] While this may be true for companies with codes, the same may be true of companies without codes. Does it necessarily follow that companies with codes are worse off than those without?

> There must be an *independent external monitoring and compliance verification system* to engender public trust and credibility in the industry's claims of performance. Performance with code compliance on the part of member companies or groups must be subjected to independent external monitoring and compliance verification. It is in this area that companies and industries offer the most resistance. It is argued that external monitoring would create an environment of distrust and policing.[61]

59 S. Prakash Sethi, ed., *Globalization and Self-Regulation: The Crucial Role That Corporate Codes of Conduct Play in Global Business* (New York: Palgrave Macmillan, 2011), at 7.
60 S. Prakash Sethi, ed., *Globalization and Self-Regulation: The Crucial Role That Corporate Codes of Conduct Play in Global Business* (New York: Palgrave Macmillan, 2011), at 11.
61 S. Prakash Sethi, ed., *Globalization and Self-Regulation: The Crucial Role That Corporate Codes of Conduct Play in Global Business* (New York: Palgrave Macmillan, 2011), at 13 (emphasis in original).

Rather than policing, it should be viewed as a form of auditing or ensuring compliance. The sanctions for a breach are not akin to the power of the state as exercised through the police. The FSC may be considered as an ideal code in that the involvement of many stakeholders was available.

> The FSC standard is widely considered to be the highest social and environmental standard in the forestry sector and across continents, forest types, sizes, and various kinds of ownerships due to its equitable approach to improving environmental, social, and economic performance.[62]

Being co-opted/selling out

Not-for-profit organizations and charities that align themselves with corporations or that are involved in corporate engagement be seen as being co-opted or termed "sellouts" by peers as well as in the media. One can look at the alliance between Coca-Cola and WWF[63] as an example of corporate engagement, which may be a public relations ploy on the part of Coca-Cola or an example of corporate philanthropy. One must again ponder whether this specific instance cannot be deemed to be in fact both. Are the two separate and distinct? Or can one action be both about public relations and philanthropy at the same time? These questions need to be examined. Does the motivation on the part of the corporation matter when choosing to donate funds to not-for-profits? Or does the end result determine success (more money to WWF)? In this example, one may say that WWF has been co-opted or is selling out their cause by aligning with corporations that may have a poor record in the environmental sphere. Then again, maybe it is in everyone's interests to think about some not-for-profits being more influenced than others (arguably WWF as opposed to Greenpeace, which holds out that it does not accept corporate funds) but in turn being more influential than others as a result. Does seeing a polar bear on a Coca-Cola can remind you that polar bears are losing their natural habitat? Is this more far reaching and arguably more influential than the work of not-for-profits who are not able to get their message out in mainstream media? Basically if a not-for-profit is "selling out" but doing so effectively, this may actually prove to increase education and awareness about issues that would otherwise be muted.

62 S. Prakash Sethi, ed., *Globalization and Self-Regulation: The Crucial Role That Corporate Codes of Conduct Play in Global Business* (New York: Palgrave Macmillan, 2011), at 194.

63 Advertising campaign underway in Fall 2011 prior to the holiday season when Coca-Cola was declaring that it would be turning its trademark red cans white in support of polar bears' habitat preservation through their alliance with WWF.

Bibliography for Chapter 3

Legislation

Bank *Act*, SC 1991, c 46.
Bankruptcy *and Insolvency Act*, RSC 1985, c B-3.
Canada *Business Corporations Act*, RSC 1985, c C-44.
Canada *Cooperatives Act*, SC 1998, c 1.
Canada *Not-for-profit Corporations Act*, SC 2009, c 23.
Insurance *Companies Act*, SC 199, c 47.
Trust *and Loan Companies Act*, SC 1991, c 45.

Caselaw

BCE Inc v 1976 Debentureholders, 2008, 3 SCR 560.
Peoples *Department Stores Inc (Trustee of) v Wise*, 2004, 3 SCR 461.

Secondary sources

Books

Divinney, Timothy M., Pat Auger, & Giana M. Eckhardt, *The Myth of the Ethical Consumer* (Cambridge: Cambridge University Press, 2010).
Murray, Jill, *Transnational Labour Regulation: The ILO and EC Compared* (Norwell: Kluwer Law International, 2001).
Novitz, Tonia & David Mangan, eds., *The Role of Labour Standards in Development: From Theory to Sustainable Practice?* (New York: Oxford University Press, 2011).
Novogratz, Jacqueline, *The Blue Sweater: Bridging the Gap Between Rich and Poor in an Interconnected World* (New York: Rodale Books, 2009).
Sethi, S. Prakash, ed., *Globalization and Self-Regulation: The Crucial Role That Corporate Codes of Conduct Play in Global Business* (New York: Palgrave Macmillan, 2011).
Sukdeo, Vanisha H., *Regulation and Inequality at Work: Isolation and Inequality Beyond the Regulation of Labour* (New York: Routledge, 2018).

Book chapters

Barrientos, Stephanie, "Mapping Codes Through the Value Chain: From Researcher to Detective" in Rhys Jenkins, Ruth Pearson, & Gill Seyfang, eds., *Corporate Responsibility and Labour Rights: Codes of Conduct in the Global Economy* (London: Earthscan Publications Limited, 2002).
Murray, Jill, "Labour Rights/Corporate Responsibilities: The Role of ILO Labour Standards" in Rhys Jenkins, Ruth Pearson, & Gill Seyfang, eds., *Corporate Responsibility and Labour Rights: Codes of Conduct in the Global Economy* (London: Earthscan Publications Limited, 2002).
Shaw, Linda & Angela Hale, "The Emperor's New Clothes: What Codes Mean for Workers in the Garment Industry" in Rhys Jenkins, Ruth Pearson, & Gill Seyfang,

eds., *Corporate Responsibility and Labour Rights: Codes of Conduct in the Global Economy* (London: Earthscan Publications Limited, 2002).

Articles

Berle, Adolf A., "For Whom Corporate Managers Are Trustees: A Note" *Harvard Law Review* vol 45 no 8 (June 1932) pp. 1365–1372.

Bradley, Sarah P., "BCE Inc. v. 1976 Debenture-Holders: The New Fiduciary Duties of Fair Treatment, Statutory Compliance and Good Corporate Citizenship?" *Ottawa Law Review* vol 41 (2009–2010) pp. 325–349.

Dhir, Aaron, "The Politics of Knowledge Dissemination: Corporate Reporting, Shareholder Voice, and Human Rights" *Osgoode Hall LJ* vol 47 (2009) pp. 47–83.

Dodd, E. Merrick, "For Whom Are Corporate Managers Trustees?" *Harvard Law Review* vol 45 no 7 (May 1932) pp. 1145–1163.

Flannigan, Robert, "Fiduciary Duties of Shareholders and Directors" *JBL* (May 2004) pp. 277–302.

McWilliams, Abigail, Donald S. Siegel, & Patrick M. Wright, "Corporate Social Responsibility: Strategic Implications" *Journal of Management Studies* vol 43 no 1 (January 2006) pp. 1–18.

Richardson, Benjamin, J., "Do the Fiduciary Duties of Pension Funds Hinder Socially Responsible Investment?" *BLFR* vol 22 no 2 (2007) pp. 145–201.

Sukdeo, Vanisha H., "What Is the Benefit of a 'Benefit Corporation'?: Examining the Advantages and Detriment" *Banking and Finance Law Review* vol 31 no 1 (2015) pp. 89–111.

VanDuzer, J. Anthony, "*BCE v 1976 Debentureholders*: The Supreme Court's Hits and Misses in Its Most Important Corporate Law Decision Since *Peoples*" *UBC Law Review* vol 43 no 1 (2010) pp. 205–258.

Websites

The State Bar of California, Business Law Section, Memo to Jared Huffman, online: <www.thecorporatecounsel.net/nonMember/docs/04_26_11_AB361.pdf> at 1.

4 Changes to standard union contracts

Codes of conduct are a separate layer of governance that does not lend itself to working in conjunction with a collective agreement. Codes exist only in the absence of collective agreements. Collective agreements exist between management and union members to protect the rights of both parties as management is allowed to grieve using the grievance process, although it is rarely used in that manner. Collective agreements usually contain a section on management rights which ensures that certain decisions are left to the sole discretion of management. Unions have responded to the new economy after the economic downturn in 2008 and have been making significant changes in both how they organize and how they negotiate new collective agreements.

Even among unions, there are differences. Some unions can be described as more "bread and butter," as the model they follow is more akin to members paying union dues and the union grieving for its members. Other unions are more social justice oriented, or activist or militant. These unions tend to be more involved in advancing the concerns of all workers and may have social justice committees, women's committees, etc.[1] Just like corporations can vary from more profit driven to more socially responsible, so too can unions vary.[2] Unions have to adapt to changes in the economy, and codes are able to exist in places where it is difficult to unionize and attaches duty to the corporation itself rather than govern the workplace in each different jurisdiction in a disorganized manner. Codes exist where there is no union and allows for the governance void to be filled by having a place for workers to exist and thrive. When one thinks about workers' voice as a collective and the voice of shareholders, these two do not have to be at odds. There is space for both.

1 Just my inside information having articled at OPSEU (a public sector union) and prior to that spending time in the legal department at then CAW (now Unifor), the largest private sector union in Canada.

2 As an aside, I recall a union organizer telling me that management "gets the union you deserve" in that management who is mean to their workers gets a more militant union, whereas management that is nice to its workers may get a more diplomatic union.

As noted in Chapter 1, the underlying theories behind corporate law and workers' rights are divergent. The competing theories about corporate law explore whether the corporation is "a nexus of contracts," whether the corporation serves the public or its shareholders, the role of agency, and whether Directors and Officers are merely agents of the shareholders. The competing theories about workers' rights are as extreme as those promulgated by Bakan and McNally to the less radical theories put forward by Fung, O'Rourke, and Sabel. These scholars explore the extent to which workers are the main vehicle in society and how much protection they deserve due to the corresponding role – if they are major vehicles, then perhaps they are more worthy of protection, and worthy of a greater level of protection, than other groups.

The importance of freedom of association and collective bargaining

UNGC

The United Nations Global Compact was developed in 2000 to try to encourage corporations to incorporate the 10 principles[3] put forth in the areas of sustainability, human rights, fair treatment for workers, and reduction of corruption. Sethi and Schepers mention that the KPCS is more transparent than other schemes.[4] They conclude that the UNGC is "long on promises, short on performance."[5]

When examining the effectiveness of codes it is not obvious that codes make a dramatic difference in advancing the rights of workers. Professor Patrick Erwin at the Center for Marine Science at the University of North Carolina Wilmington notes that a recent study indicated that over four decades of empirical research on codes, only 27 studies reported a significantly positive effect as result of codes; 13 studies reported a weak effect, 26 studies reported no significant

3 Principle 1: Business should support and respect the protection of internationally proclaimed human rights
Principle 2: Make sure that they are not complicit in human rights abuses
Principle 3: Businesses should uphold the freedom of association and the effective recognition of the right to collective bargaining
Principle 4: The elimination of all forms of forced and compulsory labour
Principle 5: The effective abolition of child labour
Principle 6: The elimination of discrimination in respect of employment and occupation
Principle 7: Businesses should support a precautionary approach to environmental challenges
Principle 8: Undertake initiatives to promote greater environmental responsibility
Principle 9: Encourage the development and diffusion of environmentally friendly techniques
Principle 10: Businesses should work against corruption in all its forms, including extortion and bribery

4 S. Prakash Sethi & Donald H. Schepers, "United Nations Global Compact: The Promise-Performance Gap" *Journal of Business Ethics* vol 122 (2014) pp. 193–208 at 197.

5 S. Prakash Sethi & Donald H. Schepers, "United Nations Global Compact: The Promise-Performance Gap" *Journal of Business Ethics* vol 122 (2014) pp. 193–208 at 207.

Table 4.1 Eight conditions that can be applied to ensure a higher level of effectiveness in codes

1	The code must be substantive in addressing broad areas of public concern pertaining to industry's conduct.
2	Code principles or standards must be specific in addressing issues embodied in those principles.
3	Code performance standards must be realistic in the context of industry's financial strength and competitive environment. The industry should not make exaggerated promises or claim implausible achievements.
4	Member companies must create an effective internal implementation system to ensure effective code compliance.
5	Code compliance must be an integral part of a management performance evaluation and reward system.
6	The industry must create an independent governance structure that is not controlled by the executives of the member companies.
7	There must be an independent external monitoring and compliance verification system to engender public trust and credibility in the industry's claims of performance.
8	There should be a maximum transparency and verifiable disclosure of industry's performance to the public. Standards of performance disclosure should be the sole province of the code's governing board.

Source: S. Prakash Sethi and Donald H Schepers, "United Nations Global Compact: The Promise-Performance Gap" *J Bus Ethics* (2014) 122: 193–208 at 198.

effects, and 11 studies produced mixed results and one negative result.[6] The study cited by Erwin was from a paper by Professor Muel Kaptein and Professor Mark S. Schwartz, where the authors include a table listing the findings of the studies they examined.[7] Kaptein and Schwartz note that business codes contain such varied language as mission statements, beliefs, values, principles, guidelines, standards, and rules.[8] Kaptein and Schwartz examine "business codes," a term they use broadly to cover codes of conduct including internal codes about employee behaviour. While it is important to use their study, it is useful to distinguish it from studies that deal only with codes of conduct, such as Locke.

> These findings may suggest that: 1) codes of conduct have positive impacts despite their content, and/or 2) codes of conduct are not a perquisite for

6 Patrick M. Erwin, "Corporate Codes of Conduct: The Effects of Code Content and Quality on Ethical Performance" *Journal of Business Ethics* vol 99 (2011) pp. 535–548 at 536.

7 Muel Kaptein & Mark S. Schwartz, "The Effectiveness of Business Codes: A Critical Examination of Existing Studies and the Development of an Integrated Research Model" *Journal of Business Ethics* vol 77 (2008) pp. 111–127.

8 Muel Kaptein & Mark S. Schwartz, "The Effectiveness of Business Codes: A Critical Examination of Existing Studies and the Development of an Integrated Research Model" *Journal of Business Ethics* vol 77 (2008) pp. 111–127 at 113.

> ethical conduct within organizations. Evidence for the first hypothesis has been reported and suggests that the sole act of establishing a formal code of conduct, regardless or content, is sufficient to impact perceptions of ethical behaviour within organizations.[9]

The authors caution that the diverging coverage regarding the topics that codes deal with, from reduction of child labour and reduction of fraud to social diversity, make it difficult to compare codes and to measure the effectiveness of codes.[10] Some of the studies merely surveyed respondents regarding their personal perceptions about the codes, which seems unusual as there could be better tools and a more objective standard to use rather than asking self-interested internal individuals. In some of the studies, items like fire exits and fire extinguishers being in factories can be used to look at the reductions in fires. It is easier to measure quantifiable changes like that. The authors propose a model for the effectiveness of business codes.

Professor Niklas Egels-Zanden (School of Business, University of Gothenberg) and Professor Henrik Lindholm (Department of Philosophy, Royal Institute of Technology) argue that codes of conduct improve worker rights on an overall level.[11] Fair Wear Foundation is a Dutch-based MSI founded in 1999 that conducts independent verification of companies' performance in line with the FWF code of conduct. They state that codes have an uneven impact, especially on increasing specific worker rights. As noted by Barrientos, codes fail "to improve process rights (such as trade union rights and discrimination)."[12] They go on to state that compliant factories may not remain compliant.[13] "Locke et al. (2007a, 2007b) used Nike's internal rating of 800 factories over time, almost half of the factories did not improve their compliance; 36% actually experienced a decline in compliance, and only approximately 20% improved."[14] Linking back to ethical consumption, some companies adopt practices that

9 Patrick M. Erwin, "Corporate Codes of Conduct: The Effects of Code Content and Quality on Ethical Performance" *Journal of Business Ethics* vol 99 (2011) pp. 535–548 at 545.

10 Muel Kaptein & Mark S. Schwartz, "The Effectiveness of Business Codes: A Critical Examination of Existing Studies and the Development of an Integrated Research Model" *Journal of Business Ethics* vol 77 (2008) pp. 111–127 at 115.

11 Niklas Egels-Zanden & Henrik Lindholm, "Do Codes of Conduct Improve Worker Rights in Supply Chains? A Study of Fair Wear Foundation" *Journal of Cleaner Production* vol 107 (2015) pp. 31–40 at 31.

12 Niklas Egels-Zanden & Henrik Lindholm, "Do Codes of Conduct Improve Worker Rights in Supply Chains? A Study of Fair Wear Foundation" *Journal of Cleaner Production* vol 107 (2015) pp. 31–40 at 32.

13 Niklas Egels-Zanden & Henrik Lindholm, "Do Codes of Conduct Improve Worker Rights in Supply Chains? A Study of Fair Wear Foundation" *Journal of Cleaner Production* vol 107 (2015) pp. 31–40 at 32.

14 Niklas Egels-Zanden & Henrik Lindholm, "Do Codes of Conduct Improve Worker Rights in Supply Chains? A Study of Fair Wear Foundation" *Journal of Cleaner Production* vol 107 (2015) pp. 31–40 at 32.

would brand them as socially responsible to attract certain consumers. Oka notes that the Better Factory Cambodia was more focused on "reputation-conscious buyers" akin to the ethical consumer.[15]

> Our results of the overall impacts of codes of conduct show that suppliers, regardless of measure, improve between the first and second audit. This finding stands in contrast to Locke et al. finding that the compliance of Nike suppliers did not improve over time.[16]

The authors note that the time difference may account for the differences in results. Locke's time period was 1998–2005, and theirs was 2002–2012. The authors conclude by stating that managers have to decide to move beyond merely compliance-based code of conduct to the more cooperative model advocated by Locke.[17] It is also considered whether codes should be abandoned in favour of another private regulatory mechanism such as certifications.

Codes versus certifications

Because of the ability of capital to cross borders in a distinct way from laws, it may be easier to regulate the corporation through codes, which traverse borders, than to bind it to national laws.

> The effect of these developments has been to give multinational corporations remarkable freedom to choose the legal systems that will govern their operations. Corporations are now free to seek out those environments in which the laws in place provide the most favourable conditions for maximizing profits.[18]

As mentioned in the previous chapter, a rule/law, such as a code, should be used that moves with the corporation and that remains in place no matter what jurisdiction the company is in. This bridges the divide between host nations and home nation, as the corporation is bound by the code no matter what border it crosses. This allows for consistency and predictability, as the code is

15 Niklas Egels-Zanden & Henrik Lindholm, "Do Codes of Conduct Improve Worker Rights in Supply Chains? A Study of Fair Wear Foundation" *Journal of Cleaner Production* vol 107 (2015) pp. 31–40 at 33.

16 Niklas Egels-Zanden & Henrik Lindholm, "Do Codes of Conduct Improve Worker Rights in Supply Chains? A Study of Fair Wear Foundation" *Journal of Cleaner Production* vol 107 (2015) pp. 31–40 at 37.

17 Niklas Egels-Zanden & Henrik Lindholm, "Do Codes of Conduct Improve Worker Rights in Supply Chains? A Study of Fair Wear Foundation" *Journal of Cleaner Production* vol 107 (2015) pp. 31–40 at 39.

18 Wesley Cragg, ed., *Ethics Codes, Corporations, and the Challenge of Globalization* (Northampton: Edward Elgar Publishing Limited, 2003), at 2.

the same in every jurisdiction, rather than trying to navigate and manage the differing employment laws that exist in different nations.

Corporations do not have the same availability of enforcement that is available to the state.

> [I]t is both valid and useful to study the ILO Conventions in their own right, independently of their ratification and implementation at the national level. The Conventions can be studied as a body of rules which reflects the views of the tripartite delegates of the ILO Member States at the International Labour Conference in any given year.[19]

Because of the malleability of the Conventions, Murray argues that they are not quite as useful as planned.

> The character of transnational labour rules of the ILO and the Community is thus at times rather difficult to capture. For the most part, they are not instruments of direct "governance," and they do not "regulate" as national legislation does. The details in international rules are often templates for multiple outcomes within and between national jurisdictions."[20]

The purpose of shareholder proposals

The corporation allows for its own reformation from within through the proposal mechanism. This allows for shareholder democracy to thrive. This also shows that the corporation is willing to be shaped on certain issues.

Shareholder proposals and codes of conduct can be linked. They can work together or separately to achieve similar results. In my research, I have found that the two mechanisms can work congruently to help increase the rights of workers. Through the proposal system, shareholders can voice their concerns, and the resulting code of conduct can be the mechanism that actually carries through the desired impact. The proposal system is important because it is the tool used as a power conveyance. Without the proposal system, the shareholder voice may be more silenced.

Different stakeholder groups may have differing priorities, which is reflected in their differing interests and focus.

> The proximity of stakeholders to a company's CR actions ranges from a complete lack of awareness of any such activities, to a central, driving role in the company's CR strategy. A fundamental goal of a company's CR strategy,

19 Jill Murray, *Transnational Labour Regulation: The ILO and EC Compared* (Norwell: Kluwer Law International, 2001), at 5.

20 Jill Murray, *Transnational Labour Regulation: The ILO and EC Compared* (Norwell: Kluwer Law International, 2001), at 7.

> then, must be to move the most important and/or valued stakeholder – employees and consumers – up this proximity continuum, from utter unawareness to complete involvement.[21]

This spectrum of very involved (perhaps overly involved) groups to the less involved is important. Some groups may have more resources or time to devote to particular causes, thus making them more involved in some companies.

> Foremost among these risks is the concern that (in contrast to communication surrounding products and services) CR communication can produce heightened skepticism about the company's intentions and even actions, causing it, at least under certain situations, to backfire on the company, in terms of negative stakeholder reactions.[22]

This means that a company that portrays itself as a CSR leader may become a target for activists or stakeholder groups. This may be a difficult position to manage – that those who put themselves out as CSR leaders may be targeted while those who are laggards manage to avoid detection.

The solution put forward by Bhattacharya, Sen, and Korschun is simple.

> Specifically, our framework suggests that in trying to optimize stakeholder reactions, companies need to have the following CR communication goals: (1) increase awareness, (2) assure credibility, (3) convey effectiveness, (4) clarify usefulness (i.e., the benefits to the stakeholders), and (5) make the company identity salient.[23]

These options will help to build a profile for a company that wants to become a CSR leader.

> In many instances, the company may find that the stakeholder is confused about the CR issues at stake, not because they are under-informed, but actually over-informed. Because of the sheer volume of often confusing and even contradictory information stakeholders are exposed to on a regular

21 C. B. Bhattacharya, Sankar Sen, & Daniel Korschun, *Leveraging Corporate Responsibility: The Stakeholder Route to Maximizing Business and Social Value* (Cambridge: Cambridge University Press, 2011), at 186.
22 C. B. Bhattacharya, Sankar Sen, & Daniel Korschun, *Leveraging Corporate Responsibility: The Stakeholder Route to Maximizing Business and Social Value* (Cambridge: Cambridge University Press, 2011), at 189.
23 C. B. Bhattacharya, Sankar Sen, & Daniel Korschun, *Leveraging Corporate Responsibility: The Stakeholder Route to Maximizing Business and Social Value* (Cambridge: Cambridge University Press, 2011), at 191.

> basis, they may either tune out or be quite at sea as to what really are the key issues and facts and why these matter.[24]

This is interesting in that with the increase of readily available technology, information production and dissemination has increased greatly. The problem may be that incorrect information is able to travel through the same channels as correct information. The internet allows for information to be widely disseminated but does not act as a filter to verify information. The average consumer or employee may not be able to discern whether information is valid. "However, providing specific numbers and also acknowledging the benefit of CR to the company itself – instead of presenting CR as entirely a good-will venture – comes off as realistic and acceptable to stakeholders."[25] Stakeholders may not expect great change but gradual and lasting change. Sudden and drastic change may not be the desired outcome, as it seems that what is won easily and quickly may not be as enduring as the change brought about gradually (whether or not it is difficult).

The problem with CSR is that it is such a new area, one in which the outcomes are rather unpredictable and difficult to measure. It does not benefit from years of history, such as law, economics, or finance.

> The first question is whether CR programs are having their intended effects. Managers need to know that their CR programs are really generating value. The second question (related to the first) is how stakeholders are interpreting CR activity. This speaks to the underlying reasoning stakeholders engage in deciding whether they want to approach or withdraw from the company.[26]

The reason for stakeholder engagement is needed as well as the desired outcome for that particular group. The need to determine whether the interest or desires are ever actualized is the next step.

Making the corporation "moral"

Activists are becoming aware that corporate power sometimes outweighs the power of the nation state.

24 C. B. Bhattacharya, Sankar Sen, & Daniel Korschun, *Leveraging Corporate Responsibility: The Stakeholder Route to Maximizing Business and Social Value* (Cambridge: Cambridge University Press, 2011), at 208.

25 C. B. Bhattacharya, Sankar Sen, & Daniel Korschun, *Leveraging Corporate Responsibility: The Stakeholder Route to Maximizing Business and Social Value* (Cambridge: Cambridge University Press, 2011), at 209.

26 C. B. Bhattacharya, Sankar Sen, & Daniel Korschun, *Leveraging Corporate Responsibility: The Stakeholder Route to Maximizing Business and Social Value* (Cambridge: Cambridge University Press, 2011), at 215.

> Activists have long noted that "lobbying the corporation" (Vogel 1978) directly is a viable alternative to targeting states. While classical social movements tried to achieve their aims through the state, transnational protest groups increasingly circumvent state politics by addressing their claims directly to transnational corporations (Spar and La Mure 2003).[27]

Industry-wide standards and codes of conduct may be alternatives to lobbying the corporation directly but rather impose a uniform standard across a variety of corporations.

Activism

Some activists may be more neutral than others. While activists are trying to change corporate behaviour, it may be the case that other activists are being co-opted. "As a result of successful activism, corporations seek to co-opt specific external interest groups. They turn new 'stakeseekers' into stakeholders and thereby reduce the uncertainties of a complex social environment."[28]

The notion of power relations is important, as it may be that corporations have more power and money than stakeholders; however, the stakeholder group such as consumers has an interest and ability to change the corporation through purchasing choices.

> This presupposes that power is something one can "possess" and therefore give or lose to someone else. Power however is always embedded in social relations and hence nobody can possess it. It always takes (at least) two to play this game – or, as Michel Foucault put it: "Power is not something that is acquired, seized, or shared, something that one holds on to or allows to slip away; power is exercised from innumerable points, in the interplay of nonegalitarian and mobile relations" (Foucault 1979: 94).[29]

This interaction between consumers and the corporation is about power flowing both ways. One group seems more powerful, the corporation, yet cannot exist without the other. This symbiotic relationship is not often discussed, as the power is usually thought to flow from the corporation itself.

> Amongst others, Lukes (1974) and Wrong (1979) have emphasized that this ability to "frame" the issue may furthermore be based upon a third,

27 Brian Holzer, *Moralizing the Corporation: Transnational Activism and Corporate Accountability* (Northampton: Edward Elgar Publishing Limited, 2010), at 3.
28 Brian Holzer, *Moralizing the Corporation: Transnational Activism and Corporate Accountability* (Northampton: Edward Elgar Publishing Limited, 2010), at 6.
29 Brian Holzer, *Moralizing the Corporation: Transnational Activism and Corporate Accountability* (Northampton: Edward Elgar Publishing Limited, 2010), at 9.

> structural dimension of power, which enables power-holders to manipulate the very structures from which situations of conflict and contest may arise.[30]

This may allow corporations to bend the power in its favour by using the media, etc., to paint activists as uninformed radicals.[31]

The ability of the law to shape corporate behaviour needs to be studied further. However, the power of the corporation itself may make it less of a regulatory target.

> Laws cannot prescribe concrete actions and are subject to interpretation. Corporations do not see legal norms as "precise normative commands requiring obedience" but rather perceive them selectively and reconstruct them "according to the inner logic of the concrete market and the concrete organization" (Teubner 1994: 33; see also Stone 1975).[32]

The corporation as selective in its choice of which law to follow may be the result of efficient breaches where it is easier to pay a fine for not complying rather than paying the cost of compliance.

> Despite the oft-cited David vs. Goliath metaphor, anti-corporate activities pose a considerable threat to TNCs. Even if one assumes that corporations actually "rule the world" (Korten 1995), their rule may well become self-defeating, as they then become a natural target for transnational social movement activities.[33]

While corporations may become greater targets for activists, that does not necessarily entail that activists are successful in reducing the power that corporations hold. Altering corporate behaviour is not the same as reducing power. While it may be said that the activists hold some power to get the corporation to change, it does not mean that the corporation's power has been reduced.

With the degradation of state-centred governance models, the move towards private regulation in the form of corporate regulation may be growing.

> In the absence of a global system of law, global norms cannot be as formal or binding as legal norms. Rather, they are part of a rather loose system of "soft law" that is produced and elaborated by means of public discourse.

30 Brian Holzer, *Moralizing the Corporation: Transnational Activism and Corporate Accountability* (Northampton: Edward Elgar Publishing Limited, 2010), at 10.

31 See Chapter 1.

32 Brian Holzer, *Moralizing the Corporation: Transnational Activism and Corporate Accountability* (Northampton: Edward Elgar Publishing Limited, 2010), at 13.

33 Brian Holzer, *Moralizing the Corporation: Transnational Activism and Corporate Accountability* (Northampton: Edward Elgar Publishing Limited, 2010), at 27.

> The fact that world society remains a stateless (and thus, in some sense: a "lawless") polity does not imply that there are no norms at all.[34]

If those in power enact laws that maintain that power, the same can be said of corporate power. If corporations hold power akin to governments, then they may be able to push off formal regulation mechanisms in favour of soft law approaches.

> Acting on behalf of the principles of world culture, however, transnational advocacy groups become sources of authority in the global realm. They cannot draw on the legal authority of nation-states but on the rational-voluntaristic authority associated with their causes and principles.[35]

This in turn allows for corporate engagement in that activists can choose to have corporations become allies in their cause. Activists must be vigilant against being co-opted.

> The way in which corporate policies affect human rights, for instance, is often more indirect. Corporations rarely arrest or torture people, but they may collude with or lend financial or other support to authoritarian regimes. The question then is how direct the connection is between the production of consumer goods and the violation of human rights in developing countries – and how political consumerism can make a difference by exerting pressure on the corporations.[36]

The example of blood diamonds in Africa has brought international attention to how corporations can help to fund civil wars in other parts of the world. This can also be said about coltan mining in Rwanda and the Congo.

> Boycott campaigns again a particular product, company or industry sector first come to mind. But they are often combined with the call to "buycott," i.e. to give preference to other goods that comply with higher environmental, ethical and social standards (cf. Friedman 1991, 1999).[37]

The notion of buycott is similar to ethical consumption in that products that are ethical become market favourites among consumers. "The framing and

34 Brian Holzer, *Moralizing the Corporation: Transnational Activism and Corporate Accountability* (Northampton: Edward Elgar Publishing Limited, 2010), at 31.
35 Brian Holzer, *Moralizing the Corporation: Transnational Activism and Corporate Accountability* (Northampton: Edward Elgar Publishing Limited, 2010), at 33.
36 Brian Holzer, *Moralizing the Corporation: Transnational Activism and Corporate Accountability* (Northampton: Edward Elgar Publishing Limited, 2010), at 42.
37 Brian Holzer, *Moralizing the Corporation: Transnational Activism and Corporate Accountability* (Northampton: Edward Elgar Publishing Limited, 2010), at 44.

branding of a corporation therefore allows transnational activism to tap the resource of 'political consumerism,' i.e. of consumers who are willing to base their shopping decisions on political or ethical criteria."[38]

Consumer autonomy

Perhaps the notion that consumers hold much sway in regard to corporate power is a fallacy.

> If the consumer wields any power at all it must derive from the ability to choose from a range of options. Yet if those options are dependent on the range of choice offered by the producers, what remains of the power and influence of the consumer? Is it a mere illusion? Or does it exist, if only in a limited and secondary form?[39]

How much power do consumers truly yield? Perhaps the power is less than originally conceived. Perhaps if one consumer chooses not to purchase one product, it does not mean that the next consumer will also refuse. This is the same problem with shareholders who sell their shares when faced with a "bad" corporation – the share still exists on the market for someone else to purchase. The reduction in overall "bad" products is not reduced in and of itself. That product stays on the shelf for someone else to purchase. "From the perspective of social movements, individual consumers 'lend' their purchasing power to them and thus enable them to establish effective threats on the marketplace."[40]

The corporation and developing countries

Governments have a role to play in regard to allowing sweatshops to exist. People may only work in sweatshops because there is a lack of jobs in their country. The eventual passage of such legislation will help to create an onus on Canadian corporations to govern their conduct in host nations similar to their conduct at home. The ability to view people as 'other' allows for less concern for their wellbeing.

Certification schemes

To examine the difference between codes of conduct and certification schemes, it is worth looking at one example – the Kimberley Process Certification Scheme.

38 Brian Holzer, *Moralizing the Corporation: Transnational Activism and Corporate Accountability* (Northampton: Edward Elgar Publishing Limited, 2010), at 62.
39 Brian Holzer, *Moralizing the Corporation: Transnational Activism and Corporate Accountability* (Northampton: Edward Elgar Publishing Limited, 2010), at 62.
40 Brian Holzer, *Moralizing the Corporation: Transnational Activism and Corporate Accountability* (Northampton: Edward Elgar Publishing Limited, 2010), at 72.

There has been much news in the mainstream media about blood diamonds, which can be described as diamonds that have been mined and transported from conflict zones such as Rwanda and the Congo. While it has been noted that the mining of diamonds in these regions has helped to fund and support armed conflict, the same attention has not been given to the mining of other conflict minerals. What is the connection between your cellphone and the atrocities in the Congo? It may be distressing to learn that coltan (columbite-tantalite) is an essential component in cellphones, smartphones, tablets, and laptops. While not all coltan is necessarily mined in the Congo, much of the world's supply can be found in that region. I will outline the problem in the Congo and how it can be reformed and will discuss the *Dodd-Frank Wall Street Reform and Consumer Protection Act* (*Dodd-Frank Act* or *Dodd-Frank*). I will then examine the Kimberley Process Certification Scheme (KPCS). The enactment of the *Dodd-Frank* provisions on conflict minerals could be a starting point to help end the trade of conflict minerals, and a similar provision could be enacted in Canada. The effectiveness of such a provision in Canada might be the best way to halt the trade of conflict minerals. Mainstream media coverage of blood diamonds as well as a Hollywood movie[41] brought attention to the funding of armed conflict as a result of the involvement with the diamond industry and led to the enactment of the KPCS. Conflict minerals need a similar solution. Workers are being exposed to poor conditions (lack of proper equipment and guidelines), environmental devastation (damage to soil and water), and the funding of armed conflict.[42] Whichever problem is deemed most egregious does not necessarily matter, as we need to curtail all of the damaging impacts. Proposed changes are intended not to eliminate the excavation of coltan, but rather to reform the process by which it is mined, and its supply chain management more broadly.

Dodd-Frank Act

Section 1502 of the *Dodd-Frank Act* deals with conflict minerals. This Act became law on July 21, 2010, and its stated purpose is to reform the trade in conflict minerals originating in the Congo.

> 1502 (a) It is the sense of Congress that the exploitation and trade of conflict minerals originating in the Democratic Republic of the Congo is helping to finance conflict characterized by extreme levels of violence in the eastern Democratic Republic of the Congo, particularly sexual- and

41 The 2006 Warner Bros. movie *Blood Diamond*, starring Leonardo DiCaprio and written by Charles Leavitt.

42 For a comprehensive summary of the link between armed conflict and coltan mining please see "Conflict Minerals: The Search for a Normative Framework" by Louise Arimatsu and Hemi Mistry (September 2012). The authors outline the wars in the Congo as well as the UN's interaction with the Congolese government.

> gender-based violence, and contributing to an emergency humanitarian situation therein, warranting the provisions of section 13(p) of the Securities Exchange Act of 1934.[43]

The new subsection of the *Securities Exchange Act* (*SEA*) speaks about due diligence regarding the sourcing and chain of custody of such minerals. "('DRC conflict free' is defined to mean the products that do not contain minerals that directly or indirectly finance or benefit armed groups in the Democratic Republic of the Congo or an adjoining country)."[44] The legislation calls for a private sector audit in order to "monitor and stop commercial activities involving the natural resources of the DRC that contribute to the activities of armed groups and human rights violations."[45] The purpose of the amendments to the *SEA* is to force U.S. companies to disclose whether certain minerals used in their products are in fact conflict minerals. The Act sets out a definition for conflict minerals. "[T]he term 'conflict mineral' means a) columbite-tantalite (coltan), cassiterite, gold, wolframite, or their derivatives."[46] The enactment of similar legislation in Canada should be considered.[47] Legislation regulating conflict minerals could be implemented in many nations that are involved in the supply chain. However, an alternative would be to attach the governance mechanism to the corporation itself which would be independent from domestic law.

Kimberley Process Certification Scheme

Introduced on November 5, 2002, in Interlaken, Switzerland, the KPCS outlines certain requirements that participants must adhere to in order to be in compliance with the certification scheme. A certificate has to accompany each shipment of rough diamonds. The country of origin as well as the country that receives the diamonds must be included. As stated in the Interlaken Declaration:

> Re-iterating our deep concern about the international trade in conflict diamonds, which can be directly linked to the fuelling of armed conflicts, the activities of rebel movements aimed at undermining or overthrowing legitimate governments and the illicit traffic in, and proliferation of, armaments especially small arms and light weapons. We are further concerned about the consequent devastating impact of such conflicts on the peace, safety and security of people in affected countries and the systematic and gross human rights violations that have been perpetrated in such conflicts;[48]

43 Available online: <http://housedocs.house.gov/rules/finserv/111_hr4173_finsrvcr.pdf>.
44 Available online: <http://housedocs.house.gov/rules/finserv/111_hr4173_finsrvcr.pdf>.
45 Available online: <http://housedocs.house.gov/rules/finserv/111_hr4173_finsrvcr.pdf>.
46 Available online: <http://housedocs.house.gov/rules/finserv/111_hr4173_finsrvcr.pdf>.
47 These provisions have been litigated and found to be unconstitutional. See *National Association of Manufacturers v SEC* (August 18, 2015).
48 Interlaken declaration, online KPCS: <www.kimberlyprocess.com>.

The Third Year Review published in November 2006 outlines the headway made by the KPCS in the first three years.

> The Kimberley Process is essentially a consulting intergovernmental mechanism operating with the support of industry and civil society aimed at excluding "conflict diamonds" from international trade channels. To achieve this goal, the KP Participants have adopted a Certification Scheme, established by a document which provides for the creation and development of an international certification scheme for rough diamonds, on the basis of national systems. The KPCS is not a legally binding document, as a matter of international law.[49]

The KPCS is a soft law mechanism used to regulate corporations in private regulation. This is also a form of self-regulation on the part of the diamond industry.

> In the case of the DRC, for example, according to the DRC's KP statistics, the value of official diamond exports rose from US$395 million in 2002, to US$771 million in 2004, and to US$896 million in the first half of 2005 alone.[50]

The KPCS is not meant to deter the diamond trade, but rather to reform it from within. Only through convincing those on the inside that the process is worthwhile will true change be achieved.

> The Kimberley Process strives to be transparent. However, it is concerned with balancing transparency and necessary confidentiality, as in the case, for example, of security requirements when dealing with politically sensitive and/or commercially valuable information relating to the trade in rough diamonds, or information that is sub-judice.[51]

One of the concerns with industry regulation is its very nature – that it is internal and may be open to manipulation. Also, with overlapping organizations, the codes get confusing and harder to make clear to those on the ground who are directly impacted.

> In October 2002, when the Kimberley Process was in its infancy, the International Diamond Manufacturers Association (IDMA) and the World Federation of Diamond Bourses (WFDB) created a voluntary system of

49 KPCS Third Year Review: <www.kimberlyprocess.com>, at 3.
50 KPCS Third Year Review: <www.kimberlyprocess.com>, at 22.
51 KPCS Third Year Review: <www.kimberlyprocess.com>, *Ibid* at 70.

> self-regulation which required its members to sign on to a System of Warranties and a Code of Conduct.[52]

There are also other "competing" schemes and organizations such as No Dirty Gold,[53] and the Responsible Jewellery Council.[54] More uniformity and consistency throughout the industry would lead to less confusion and more transparent rules.

The technology industry's response

The response from the technology industry has been modest.

> When the link between armed groups and the DRC's minerals trade was first raised by NGOs and the UN in 2001, the electronics industry responded with promises of ethical sourcing. However, change has been too slow, and some IT companies maintain that their supply chains are too far removed to understand or too complex to manage effectively because of the sheer number of actors involved.[55]

This disavowal of control over the process allows companies to refute any responsibility. The argument that processes are too complex should not be tolerated.

> Companies can't solve this issue alone, but have a critical role to play to be part of the solution. Investors, in turn, can work collaboratively to leverage their influence to push for industry best practices on supply chain transparency and accountability. Specifically, investors should engage directly with companies and peers, and join existing coalitions or initiatives. It is also critical that companies and investors consider leveraging their knowledge in public policy involvement.[56]

This power can be shown through shareholder proposals and other shareholder democracy tools. The best way forward for conflict minerals may be to implement a certification scheme similar to KPCS.

52 KPCS Third Year Review: <www.kimberlyprocess.com>, *Ibid* at 72.
53 See website: <http://nodirtygold.earthworksaction.org/>.
54 See website: <www.responsiblejewellery.com/>.
55 Azadeh Sabour, "Complicity in the Congo: Investor Risk in the Minerals Supply Chain" *Sustainalytics*, Aug. 2010, online: <www.sustainalytics.com/sites/default/files/Complicity_in_the_Congo_Sustainalytics_FINAL_0.pdf>, at 7.
56 Azadeh Sabour, "Complicity in the Congo: Investor Risk in the Minerals Supply Chain" *Sustainalytics*, Aug. 2010, online: <www.sustainalytics.com/sites/default/files/Complicity_in_the_Congo_Sustainalytics_FINAL_0.pdf>, at 26.

> The Federal Bureau of Geo-Sciences and Natural Resources of Germany (BGR) and the Congolese government, specifically the Ministry of Mines, have partnered to create a minerals certification system for coltan, cassiterite, wolframite and gold called the Certified Trading Chains (CTC). The CTC intends to improve transparency and accountability in the mining industry's supply chain through third-party auditing of specific mine sites.[57]

Numerous different certification models may create confusion. While a more streamlined process may limit choices in governance, it would offer greater consistency and lessen confusion. Making rules and laws that are easy to understand and thus facilitate compliance should be the goal rather than unnecessary rule-making which may be viewed as busy work. One model described by Sabour outlines the supply chain:

Electronics' supply chain

1 The Mines – Armed groups control over 50% of the 200 total mines in eastern Congo.
2 Trading Houses – Minerals are transported to trading houses, most of which are not registered with the governing trading association.
3 Exporters – Exporters buy minerals from trading houses and sell them to metals traders in international markets.
4 Transit Countries – Exporters also work with buying houses in neighbouring transit countries, who then export minerals to refineries.
5 Refiners: Minerals to Metals – Importers refine unprocessed minerals into metals and sell to world market.
6 Electronics Components – Electronics companies purchase refined metals and use them for product parts.[58]

Sabour outlines how there might be risk to investors who choose to invest in conflict minerals. Although the corporation provides great protection to investors through the separation of ownership and control, investors may be more exposed to risk rather than being protected by the corporate veil. More cases about corporate law leaning towards the stakeholder model of corporate governance may lead to increased risk exposure to investors, in particular shareholders.

While it may be true that some countries have lower labour standards than other countries, it may still amount to some blame being assigned to the

57 Azadeh Sabour, "Complicity in the Congo: Investor Risk in the Minerals Supply Chain" *Sustainalytics*, Aug. 2010, online: <www.sustainalytics.com/sites/default/files/Complicity_in_the_Congo_Sustainalytics_FINAL_0.pdf>, at 16.

58 Azadeh Sabour, "Complicity in the Congo: Investor Risk in the Minerals Supply Chain" *Sustainalytics*, Aug. 2010, online: <www.sustainalytics.com/sites/default/files/Complicity_in_the_Congo_Sustainalytics_FINAL_0.pdf>, at 8.

corporation that exploits these differences by looking for countries that have lower wages in order to perhaps employ the most vulnerable workers. Codes of conduct and industry-wide standards, along with certification schemes, are trying to bring all corporations and organizations up to a minimum certain standard. "The argument that customary international law, interpreted broadly, should be used to say that multinationals are exploiting workers in the poor countries is therefore open to serious criticism."[59] The fact that Bhagwati is arguing against some worldwide standard seems confusing. Perhaps the economic argument favours free markets and these standards would hamper that.

> National mandatory codes have been proposed to complement the Global Compact and the voluntary codes. These codes, and the rules and regulations that define at home what the corporations cannot do as good citizens, would extend to a nation's multinational operations abroad.[60]

However, there must be some way to respect the rights of workers and at the most basic, their dignity. There should be rules in place that prevent the corporation from leaving its nation state in search of lower wages and lower working standards. "The edifice of corporate social responsibility, however, must rest on two foundations. One has to be altruism, which deals with what corporations *should* do. But the other must deal with regulation that defines what corporations *should not* do."[61]

Bill C-486

This is an issue for North American and European governments as well, not just a South or East problem. The current Bill being debated in the Canadian Parliament might be one method of getting to success. Bill C-486 – *An Act respecting corporate practices relating to the extraction, processing, purchase, trade and use of conflict minerals from the Great Lakes Region of Africa*[62] – which has the support of the Hon. Paul Dewar,[63] may be important in helping to regulate Canadian companies working in other jurisdictions. Dewar's Just Minerals campaign also notes that child labour may be used in the extraction and processing

59 Jagdish Bhagwati, *In Defense of Globalization* (New York: Oxford University Press, 2007), *Ibid* at 178.

60 Jagdish Bhagwati, *In Defense of Globalization* (New York: Oxford University Press, 2007), *Ibid* at 194.

61 Jagdish Bhagwati, *In Defense of Globalization* (New York: Oxford University Press, 2007), *Ibid* at 191 (emphasis in original).

62 See Bill C-486, *An Act Respecting Corporate Practices Relating to the Extraction, Processing, Purchase, Trade and Use of Conflict Minerals from the Great Lakes Region of Africa*, online: <www.parl.gc.ca/HousePublications/Publication.aspx?Language=E&Mode=1&DocId=6062040&File=4&Col=1>.

63 See Paul Dewar website: <http://pauldewar.ndp.ca/campaigns>.

of conflict minerals. While worker abuses in other countries should not be tolerated at all, such abuses are more horrendous when inflicted upon children.

It is important to note how the wording of the Bill differs from that of *Dodd-Frank*. In the Preamable, it states:

> Whereas Canada recognizes that the illegal exploitation and trading of gold, cassiterite, wolframite and coltan and their derivatives, such as tin, tungsten and tantalum, can be directly linked to the fuelling of armed conflict and to the funding of armed groups engaged in illegal activities or serious human rights abuses in the Great Lakes Region of Africa;
>
> Whereas Canada recognizes that these conflicts have devastating impacts on the peace, safety and security of people in the countries of the Great Lakes Region of Africa; . . .[64]

The jurisdiction covered by the Bill is more expansive than *Dodd-Frank* as well. The Bill makes reference to the OECD guidelines in this area, but it should be noted that having legislation that is tied to external standards can be problematic. If those external standards change, then the dependent legislation has to be adjusted accordingly. Also, being too reliant on other codes and regulations may be too interconnected in a way that is not effective. Having legislation that stands on its own can be seen as more secure as well. The end goal should be the regulation of Canadian companies when operating in other nations, so the rules that bind them in Canada should be similar elsewhere. The staggering or two-tier system that currently exists needs to be reformed. The Bill is not too onerous as it contains five clauses. The wording in *Dodd-Frank* is lengthier. However, the law as it is written can be different from how it is enforced. Only through strong enforcement mechanisms and the encouragement of compliance will any legislation on this topic really prove effective.

FSC

The FSC is often thought to be the leading standard. Its logo is featured on everything from envelopes to office paper to lumber. The amount of hectares of forest areas keeps increasing. The notion that self-regulation is indeed voluntary may be challenged, as the pressure to sign up for certain certifications, etc., may be a result of coercion.

Codes are varied, as some are stricter than others. The stricter a code, the more difficult it may be to implement it. My experience at Queen's getting the University to implement a code was informative. We started Queen's Students

64 See Bill C-486, *An Act Respecting Corporate Practices Relating to the Extraction, Processing, Purchase, Trade and Use of Conflict Minerals from the Great Lakes Region of Africa*, online: <www.parl.gc.ca/HousePublications/Publication.aspx?Language=E&Mode=1&DocId=6062040&File=4&Col=1>.

Against Sweatshops (QSAS) with the intention of having the WRC be the monitoring agency and were successful in that, but had to sacrifice certain provisions in order to get the code drafted. The pressures on advocacy groups (QSAS could fall under this umbrella) to conform or accept concessions is strong. What is better – having a weaker code that gets implemented, or holding out for a stronger one to possibly be implemented in the future? Concessions have to be accepted, and the push for a stronger code in the future must be brought about later. A starting-out point is an important one. None of us viewed our code as one that was compromised compared to other Universities. We were proud to get one implemented and were happy that it did not take very long for this progress to be made. There is not much research on the use of self-monitoring, such as Nike does. "Little research exists on the impacts of codes of conduct and self-monitoring on actual labor conditions. Nike naturally asserts that they respond effectively and sufficiently to labor concerns."[65] The Queen's Code references ILO Conventions 138, 182, and 155 and Recommendation 164. Also ILO Conventions 87, 98, and 135 are mentioned. As Sethi states, an independent external monitoring system builds public trust. Thus a code without a monitoring agency is rather purposeless.

Other monitoring agencies besides WRC and FLA

Verité

While this organization is not a monitoring agency, it is worth listing near the WRC and FLA. This is a Canadian organization that proclaims that it is working for the rights of workers. It is not a monitoring agency like the WRC and FLA.

Maquila Solidarity Network

Maquila Solidarity Network runs the "No Sweat" campaign along with Students Against Sweatshops – Canada and UNITE HERE. This organization works to help strengthen the rights of workers. This is mainly accomplished through education and awareness programs.

Behind the Label (UNITE HERE)

This campaign, which was started by UNITE HERE, works to help strengthen the rights of workers. This is mainly accomplished through education and

65 Charles Sabel, Dara O'Rourke, & Archon Fung, "Ratcheting Labor Standards: Regulation for Continuous Improvement in the Global Workplace" online: <http://papers.ssrn.com/sol3/papers.cfm?abstract_id=253833>, at 22.

awareness programs. "The textile workers' union (UNITE), as well as the yarn and fabric sectors, also began to splinter into different directions."[66]

Clean Clothes Campaign

This is an organization that originated in Europe. See Chapter 2 for more discussion on this.

Oxfam

There is a program run by Oxfam that helps to fight sweatshops. Oxfam is also part of the No Sweat campaign.

Companies that sell sweatshop free apparel

Companies that sell "sweatshop free," or "no sweat," apparel are able to attract ethical consumers. Ethical consumers are persons who are informed about their purchases and make purchasing decisions based on their ethics.

Ethical threads

No sweat apparel

There is a company, "No Sweat Apparel,"[67] which claims that their apparel is "100% union-made and 100% sweatshop free."

Better Thinking

There is an organization called Better Thinking that also manufactures ethical clothes. Rivoli notes, "On a trip to Europe, I met Mark Holt and Mike Betts of Better Thinking, a U.K. company that designed and sells and Perfect T-Shirt (perfect, that is, from an environmental and labor perspective)."[68]

Criticism of CSR

While codes may not be the best way forward in securing or increasing the rights of workers, it may prove to be partially useful. This may be a realist or

66 Pietra Rivoli, *The Travels of a T-Shirt in the Global Economy Second Edition: An Economist Examines the Markets, Power, and Politics of World Trade* (Hoboken: John Wiley & Sons, Inc., 2009), at 168.

67 No Sweat Apparel website: <www.nosweatapparel.com/>.

68 Pietra Rivoli, *The Travels of a T-Shirt in the Global Economy Second Edition: An Economist Examines the Markets, Power, and Politics of World Trade* (Hoboken: John Wiley & Sons, Inc., 2009), at 187.

cynical view. With the rise of capitalism and what may be termed "corporatism," workers must be willing to acknowledge that power and gain strength in their collective ability to speak truth to power. Only through engaging with corporations will workers be able to forge ahead. The antiquated notion that workers should be more aggressive in order to secure greater rights is a remnant of the past. The labour movement in many forms has accepted this new mode and has adapted as a result. The way forward for workers, be they union members or not, is through corporate engagement. This may be a bleak reality to accept for those veterans of the labour movement, but only by facing reality will change be made.

Bibliography for Chapter 4

Legislation

Bill C-486, An Act Respecting Corporate Practices Relating to the Extraction, Processing, Purchase, Trade and Use of Conflict Minerals from the Great Lakes Region of Africa, online: <www.parl.gc.ca/HousePublications/Publication.aspx?Language=E&Mode=1&DocId=6062040&File=4&Col=1>.

Secondary sources

Books

Bhagwati, Jagdish, *In Defense of Globalization* (New York: Oxford University Press, 2007).

Bhattacharya, C. B. Sankar Sen, & Daniel Korschun, *Leveraging Corporate Responsibility: The Stakeholder Route to Maximizing Business and Social Value* (Cambridge: Cambridge University Press, 2011).

Cragg, Wesley, ed., *Ethics Codes, Corporations, and the Challenge of Globalization* (Northampton: Edward Elgar Publishing Limited, 2003).

Holzer, Brian, *Moralizing the Corporation: Transnational Activism and Corporate Accountability* (Northampton: Edward Elgar Publishing Limited, 2010).

Murray, Jill, *Transnational Labour Regulation: The ILO and EC Compared* (Norwell: Kluwer Law International, 2001).

Rivoli, Pietra, *The Travels of a T-Shirt in the Global Economy Second Edition: An Economist Examines the Markets, Power, and Politics of World Trade* (Hoboken: John Wiley & Sons, Inc., 2009).

Articles

Egels-Zanden, Niklas & Henrik Lindholm, "Do Codes of Conduct Improve Worker Rights in Supply Chains? A Study of Fair Wear Foundation" *Journal of Cleaner Production* vol 107 (2015) pp. 31–40.

Erwin, Patrick M., "Corporate Codes of Conduct: The Effects of Code Content and Quality on Ethical Performance" *Journal of Business Ethics* vol 99 (2011) pp. 535–548.

Kaptein, Muel & Mark S. Schwartz, "The Effectiveness of Business Codes: A Critical Examination of Existing Studies and the Development of an Integrated Research Model" *Journal of Business Ethics* vol 77 (2008) pp. 111–127.

Sabel, Charles, Dara O'Rourke, & Archon Fung, "Ratcheting Labor Standards: Regulation for Continuous Improvement in the Global Workplace", online: <http://papers.ssrn.com/sol3/papers.cfm?abstract_id=253833>.

Sabour, August 2010. "Complicity in the Congo: Investor Risk in the Minerals Supply Chain", *Sustainalytics*, online: <www.sustainalytics.com/sites/default/files/Complicity_in_the_Congo_Sustainalytics_FINAL_0.pdf>.

Sethi, S. Prakash and Donald H. Schepers, "United Nations Global Compact: The Promise-Performance Gap" *Journal of Business Ethics* vol 122 (2014) pp. 193–208.

Websites

Dodd-Frank Act, online: <http://housedocs.house.gov/rules/finserv/111_hr4173_finsrvcr.pdf>.

KPCS Third Year Review, <www.kimberlyprocess.com>.

No Dirty Gold, website: <http://nodirtygold.earthworksaction.org/>.

No Sweat Apparel, website: <www.nosweatapparel.com/>.

Paul Dewar, website: <http://pauldewar.ndp.ca/campaigns>.

Responsible Jewelry, website: <www.responsiblejewellery.com/>.

5 Concluding chapter

I have observed that while hard law plays a very important role in the regulation of corporations, soft law works alongside to create a more complete framework. The decline of state-centred governance has created a governance gap. This has allowed corporations to self-regulate as a way to stave off regulation from the state or another entity. While self-regulation is often critiqued as less rigorous than state regulation, it may not be the case that it is less effective and/or efficient. Notions like the "social license to operate" have created a more nuanced approach to regulation, as regulation becomes more about appeasing those who are being impacted by the work of the corporation and less so about those in control (be it government officials, etc.). I examined codes of conduct, expanding fiduciary duties in the corporate realm, how union contracts have been changed, as well as shareholder proposals. I have surmised that codes of conduct, with a strong monitoring agency to ensure compliance, are the best device to use in order to strengthen the rights of workers.

Workers' rights are often included in corporate codes of conduct, so this new way of regulating the corporation internally through its own code allows for increased protection for workers. There are many ways to change a corporation for the better and to make it function in line with CSR principles. I chose to ground my research in corporate governance as there are various routes to increasing the rights or workers, and the one I chose to study is the internal mechanism of a corporation, codes of conduct, rather than external governance mechanisms (the work of NGOs, unions, etc.). Codes of conduct serve a similar purpose of increasing or strengthening the rights of workers in that they govern corporate behaviour in regard to labour-related issues. Although codes of conduct do not offer the force that hard law mechanisms do, they can be drafted and enforced in such a manner that reflects hard law's command. Acting outside of hard law allows workers to craft workplace environment regulations that fit their individual workplace. It also allows for increased workers' rights in jurisdictions where it is difficult to unionize or where workers choose/would rather have a code of conduct rather than belong to a union.

My model code of conduct

My proposed model code of conduct would hold corporations to a high standard and includes references to ILO Conventions which allows the code to be part of a bigger blueprint for socially responsible corporations. To ensure compliance and enforcement of the code of conduct requires a mechanism that monitors the corporation. This is best done by an external monitoring agency such as WRC which, when compared to the FLA, seems superior due to its conducting factory audits rather than relying on another party to do so. Perhaps the ideal might be to have one code of conduct that is monitored by two monitoring agencies in that they act as check and balance. This may prove to be more expensive than merely having one monitoring agency but would demonstrate a higher level of commitment to the code that is worthy of praise. A rigorous code that is well enforced by an external monitoring agency or two monitoring agencies seems to be the best level of assurance. When a corporation adopts a code of conduct, this demonstrates an aspiration to be more socially responsible but only when there is a monitoring scheme will there be true dedication to the code itself. Without a mechanism in place to ensure compliance, the code itself is rather futile.

Codes of conduct allow for greater flexibility as workers could be involved at the initial negotiation stage and on to drafting. Contrasted with a collective agreement, the process might be similar in that union members are involved with the negotiation and the drafting of the collective agreement. The difference may be that in the unionized setting where there are collective agreements, there is often a template from which a new collective agreement is based upon, such as when lawyers draft a contract from a precedent document. However, in the environment I envision, it might be that the corporation, with its own group of workers, is starting from first principles in regards to drafting its code of conduct. In the unionized setting, the staff from the union, in the form of stewards, have expertise that they bring to the table when working with the employer. In the corporate setting when a code is being implemented, this freedom from routine behaviour allows for greater flexibility regarding what can be included in the code or what can be left out. Union contracts can be formulaic, while in contrast, codes can be tailor made to fit each individual workplace.

My proposed code of conduct outlines such basic rights as the information about maximum working hours, ventilation systems in factories, and remuneration which are typical items to be found in a collective agreement but go beyond a collective agreement by encouraging employers to create an environment in which workers feel appreciated and their voice is acknowledged. This goes beyond legal structures and touches on psychological studies about inclusion in the workplace versus exclusion.[1] Professor Jane O'Reilly notes that ostracism

1 Jane O'Reilly, "Is Negative Attention Better Than No Attention? The Comparative Effects of Ostracism and Harassment at Work" online: <http://pubsonline.informs.org/doi/abs/10.1287/orsc.2014.0900>.

removes interactional dynamic and potential for exchange.[2] By not allowing workers to voice their concerns, management is not able to fully engage with the workers about potential ways to improve the workplace for *everyone*. Workers may see ways to improve productivity, etc., that management may not be able to witness without being on the shop floor. To be able to control the process without having the process control you can be rewarding for workers in a way that simple wage increases would not. In the same way that employee stock options can help get employees to become more invested in the company, so too can workers who simply feel more appreciated at work help the company to become more productive. It may be argued that an invested worker is a more loyal and devoted worker. This drive could help the worker become more valuable to the organization. In the absence of these improvements, the workers may become stagnant and less willing to devote their time and energy to the organization in a way that a respected worker might.

My model of conduct of conduct allows for a company to take a basic outline and build on it to make it work for their particular workplace. I chose the strictest aspects of the four codes I examined to come up with the most rigorous code. This code allows for workers to have their rights protected in an environment that respects their rights and freedoms. While there are other codes or models proposed by various authors, my code is detailed and exacting. Other codes may outline what should be included but do not actually detail the language (see Sabel, O'Rourke, and Fung). I think that using the code I propose coupled with the model outlined by Kaptein about constant feedback allows for a code that can change and respond to the needs of the workers. Once a code is in place, it should not be stagnant; instead, it should become stronger and more robust as times goes on – it is malleable. The principles created by Janda et al and the one devised by Sethi set out a framework to show what underlying rules should be included in codes. This leads to a discussion about rules-based versus principles-based regulation. In this example, it is a rules-based code, but there should be acknowledgement that the rules are based on far-reaching principles about respect, dignity, and safety for workers. Also related to constant improvement is the model created by Locke about workers being able to voice their concerns and have the code respond accordingly.

There could be the possibility of creating a new monitoring agency that is superior to both the FLA and the WRC. Leaving aside the option of creating a more rigorous code of conduct that may provide greater depth on specific areas, or one that is greater in breadth than the original code, it could be advantageous to have a stricter compliance mechanism. One way to guarantee compliance may be to develop a new monitoring agency that would be superior

2 Jane O'Reilly, "Is Negative Attention Better Than No Attention? The Comparative Effects of Ostracism and Harassment at Work" online: <http://pubsonline.informs.org/doi/abs/10.1287/orsc.2014.0900>.

to both the WRC and FLA. Such a monitoring agency may conduct more unplanned factory visits, may examine factories in areas that others do not, and may speak to more workers individually about their work experience. Being able to speak with individual workers in a setting off site may allow for workers to speak more openly about their workplace environment than a short chat on site. This new theorized agency could also improve by being cheaper to sign on with than the competing agencies. Making the fees lower may encourage companies with merely a code of conduct in place to sign on with a monitoring agency as well. It is still important to continue to monitor the monitors to make sure that their report findings are accurate and reliable. Without a strong monitoring agency whose reports are dependable, the system as a whole will be lacking a crucial element. Without a strong monitoring agency, the code of conduct is left to stand separately and not be examined – this allows for the code to possibly not be complied with or even ignored altogether. For workers to be protected, a safeguard must be put in place to guarantee that their rights are being protected according to the code, and breaches of the code or non-compliance should be detected and allowed to be remedied before any other action is taken.

Fiduciary duties

My suggestion that the *CBCA* be amended to include language from *Peoples* could help the Court be more standardized in its approach to making decisions in the corporate realm. Outlining the actual stakeholders that should be satisfied by borrowing such language allows Directors and Officers to know to whom they will be held accountable. It is better to use exact language rather than vague terms that have to be complied with. This language would detail towards which groups or entities the corporation is held to have a duty.

Expanding the fiduciary duties of a corporation would allow those fighting for rights in regards to corporate behaviour to have a greater claim to such rights as they would be statutory mechanisms rather than unclear ideals. Codifying such language gives greater strength and shows society that these are the principles or values that we expect corporations to comply with. Codification signals to the corporation, those who commit wrongs, and society at large that there is certain importance to be given to all stakeholders and not just to shareholders.

Benefit Corporations have an increased fiduciary duty attached to the corporation itself from its very formation. This suits the Benefit Corporation as it has many other processes in place that work in conjunction to increase or elevate the duties to stakeholders. An increase in fiduciary duties in the typical for-profit corporation may not be as successful without the same support system.

The expansion of fiduciary duties, while useful, is not the best way forward because corporations would still be able to say that importance was given to all stakeholders but the proof of such statement would be near impossible to verify. Coupled with the business judgment rule, corporations would still be able to have ultimate control without much consequence for not complying. How such compliance would be measured or ascertained would be difficult.

Shareholder proposals

Shareholder proposals, while important, do not demonstrate the initial power I attributed to them in that they are still soft law mechanisms which the corporation can choose to sweep aside. The voting success rate was quite low for most of the shareholder proposals that I examined. Also, it would be difficult to prove causation for the impact of shareholder proposals rather than mere correlation. While valuable, shareholder proposals in my research for the purpose of increasing the rights of workers merely act as a conduit through which shareholders can get the corporation to pay attention to an issue through the shareholder proposal mechanism. Once the mechanism is used, and even if successful, the end is not done; instead, the proposal requests that the corporation perform an action such as enact a code of conduct. Having a proposal be successful is not enough, and follow-through is needed. As explained elsewhere, having a code of conduct is hollow without a mechanism that ensures compliance with the code.

Steps needed for a shareholder proposal to get a code enacted

1 Shareholder proposal is put forward. →
2 If successful, then it requests the corporation to enact a code of conduct. →
3 The code gets enacted →
4 There should be a monitoring agency in place to ensure compliance with the code.
5 The monitoring agency should report back to the corporation about its findings.

This is a multi-step process, and the first step of the filing of the shareholder proposal is not as important as originally postulated. The corporation can choose to adopt a code of conduct without having the idea introduced through the shareholder proposal process. In the context of my research, the shareholder proposal is not very useful for increasing the rights of workers. The code of conduct is the best way forward.

Transnational governance

My work on transnational governance models looks at codes of conduct and monitoring agencies as tools to be used to increase the rights of workers.

> Codes are a soft law mechanism that may be used to create a voluntary standard or set of rules to which corporations are bound. While this may be viewed as rather insubstantial compared to legislation, codes have value

> in terms of allowing the two (or more) parties that are bound by the code to have direct input in drafting the code. While the inherent imbalance of power involved in the dynamics of the employment relationship between management and workers must be acknowledged and must have an impact on the creation of the code, it does allow for involvement at a level which legislation does not.[3]

The purpose is to strengthen workers' rights through codes, and this can be accomplished by either internal or external sources – legislation being external, or the corporation can amend internally through the adoption of a code of conduct. Strengthening voluntary codes of conduct is the hardening of soft law, which means the move from soft law to hard law. "Once codes are implemented their force and effect comes form having external monitoring agencies that are paid to monitor compliance."[4] The competing monitoring agencies examined in this book were the Fair Labor Association (FLA) and the Worker Rights Consortium (WRC).

The step in between state control and private regulation is consumer regulation.

> In the model I term "consumer regulation" the regulation of consumer goods is left to consumers themselves. While codes and certification agencies allow for compliance with a certain level of standards, they also create a corresponding obligation on consumers. If these codes and certifications exist in the world where consumers purchases goods and services, is the obligation not placed on consumers to be knowledgeable about these codes and certifications?[5]

I go on to discuss how codes of conduct are rather malleable, as they can be altered by future amendments to the code itself. This can be viewed as a positive aspect, as codes can be improved in later years to become more competitive, especially if competitors adopt similar codes. This may create competition between companies for the "most rigorous code" when trying to attract ethical consumers. Codes can be altered in a way that static certifications may not. This forces corporations to become CSR leaders rather than mere laggards.

3 Vanisha H. Sukdeo, "Transnational Governance Models: Codes of Conduct and Monitoring Agencies as Tools to Increase Workers' Rights" *German Law Journal* vol 13 no 12 (2012) pp. 1559–1570 at 1559.
4 Vanisha H. Sukdeo, "Transnational Governance Models: Codes of Conduct and Monitoring Agencies as Tools to Increase Workers' Rights" *German Law Journal* vol 13 no 12 (2012) pp. 1559–1570 at 1561.
5 Vanisha H. Sukdeo, "Transnational Governance Models: Codes of Conduct and Monitoring Agencies as Tools to Increase Workers' Rights" *German Law Journal* vol 13 no 12 (2012) pp. 1559–1570 at 1564.

As noted by Professor Larry Cata Backer, codes of conduct do not share the special characteristics of hard law (perhaps a more comprehensive enforcement structure) but they also do not suffer the weakness of law: "They reflect a potentially enforceable private law among the parties consenting thereto, provide a more robust basis in consent legitimacy than that offered by the more remote process of law making."[6] He goes on to state that "Corporate Codes and soft law generally are criticized as undemocratic, as dangerous because of asymmetries in bargaining power and in the difficulty of using the mechanics of state power to enforce. More importantly, soft law is viewed, like contract, as party specific and thus of little help when attempting to harmonize conduct norms over large groups of enterprises and individuals."[7] Many different codes acting in isolation can one day become industry-wide standards, and then true change can be actualized on a large scale. The idea of creating uniformity across industries in a global sense may be more productive than changing domestic laws in separation from others. Attaching the governance at the site of the corporation will force that corporation to comply with the code in any jurisdiction, as opposed to getting various laws to become standardized simultaneously.

Backer states that

> consent based governance regime among the parties may be more democratic than law as the product of interest group bargaining and strategic consideration that may or may not permit sufficient engagement by those objects of legislation who will have to bear most of its costs.[8]

As I note in the article,

> the divide between which monitoring agencies unions and other advocacy groups choose to align with speaks volumes as to which entities are more corporate driven (and perhaps controlled) than others. A lenient monitoring agency will not provide effective services in that its role is to ensure compliance with the code not merely act as a façade.[9]

The monitoring agencies that are used to enforce the codes visit factories in the case of WRC to check that companies are complying with the code. A mechanism is in place to make sure that companies adhere to the code of

6 Larry Cata Backer Blog Post on September 21, 2013, online: <http://lcbackerblog.blogspot.ca/2013/09/changing-corporate-behavior-through.html>.

7 Larry Cata Backer Blog Post on September 21, 2013, online: <http://lcbackerblog.blogspot.ca/2013/09/changing-corporate-behavior-through.html>.

8 Larry Cata Backer Blog Post on September 21, 2013, online: <http://lcbackerblog.blogspot.ca/2013/09/changing-corporate-behavior-through.html>.

9 Vanisha H. Sukdeo, "Transnational Governance Models: Codes of Conduct and Monitoring Agencies as Tools to Increase Workers' Rights" *German Law Journal* vol 13 no 12 (2012) pp. 1559–1570 at 1569.

conduct. Similar to any enforcement tool, there must be a penalty when there is a breach, and this penalty will vary from code to code depending on the language contained therein.

My work on Benefit Corporations shows yet another example of the hardening of soft law and how to use codes as a tool in corporate governance. Beyond merely abiding by the law, the need for corporations to give true weight to being socially responsible can be demonstrated through various ways. Balancing competing interests may be achieved in the non-fiduciary realm, but when discussing dual fiduciary duties, an apparent conflict arises. How is a Director to decide which stakeholders' interest will trump other stakeholders? Do profits win over the environment? Do profits win over workers? This balancing could lead to problems. It is trite to say that legislation on the books needs to be tested in the courts, but it is true that caselaw will help to interpret and understand the true limits of fiduciary duties in corporations' legislation. "It is poignantly clear that a duty premised upon fidelity, serving two or more parties may be a breach of duty."[10] How is a Director able to balance what seems to be dual fiduciary duties? It seems to be a paradox to ask someone to serve with the utmost fidelity while balancing seemingly contradicting interests. It can be expected that future caselaw will help to set parameters on the duties of Directors of corporations and will make *BCE* clearer.

Benefit Corporations are a new corporate form but do not change the overall nature of the firm. The corporate form does not change, but this new form allows for yet another alternative to exist in law. The corporation can be a Benefit Corporation from its beginnings, or choose to become a Benefit Corporation after being incorporated.

CSR is very much linked with the stakeholder model as greater corporate accountability will be able to satisfy stakeholders to a greater degree. Rather than pitting shareholder primacy against the stakeholder model it may be the case that the shareholder primacy model is being changed or amended to be more in line with the stakeholder model. Even the example of *BCE* shows how Canadian corporate law is becoming more aligned with stakeholder theory. An amalgamation of the two models may be emerging as a new model, rather than the two models being separate and distinct. Two competing models may be better served by the addition of another model that encapsulates the best parts of both and offers a viable one for moving forward. The awareness of citizens about issues in the area of CSR is one way that change is being made – from the grassroots rather than from the top down. Mainstream media coverage about such issues as workers' rights in Bangladesh to conflict minerals in the Congo is raising awareness among citizens.

I also discuss the notion "Arm's Length Exploitation" which I use to describe the phenomenon of companies that while not directly exploiting workers, they

10 Mark Ellis, *Fiduciary Duties in Canada, Looseleaf* (Toronto: Carswell, 2011), at para. 1–8.01.

hire/contract with/outsource, etc., with others who do exploit workers (the direct exploiters). This allows company A to escape liability because they are the not the actual wrongdoers, but they hire/contract with/outsource, etc. with company B, who are the direct exploiters.

CSR is often interconnected with business ethics, notions of good corporate citizenship, and issues of morality and ethics more broadly. Activists are beginning to understand that the corporation may hold power that sometimes rivals the nation state's power. In order to effect change, it may be more lasting and effective to change corporate behaviour than state behaviour. Industry-wide standards and codes of conduct may be alternatives to lobbying the corporation directly but rather impose a uniform standard across a variety of corporations. This would allow for consistency across the corporations that adopt a similar code. This may increase the strength of the workers with the ability to align their interests with those of other workers. Union negotiators employ the tactic of getting certain items included in one CA so that they can use that as a bargaining chip in a separate round of negotiations with another employer – to drive the second employer into adopting the items agreed on by the first employer.

My original hypothesis was that while codes of conduct may be effective tools in strengthening the rights of workers, they are but a few tools among many available, and that many tools being used at the same time for the same purpose will prove more effective than a single tool. I have demonstrated that codes of conduct are an effective tool in increasing the rights of workers. When paired with a monitoring agency that is rigourous and conducts spot audits in factories, they create a scheme that very much models hard law with the code being akin to legislation and the monitoring agency being like the government to enforce the code. This is particularly helpful in jurisdictions where it is difficult to unionize. Within jurisdictions where unionizing is not difficult, the code of conduct model offers greater malleability than legislation and other hard law mechanisms. The ability for a code of conduct to reflect the voice of workers may be greater than that within a unionized context where it may be said to be more rigid than the flexible code which can be altered from one corporation to another. There maybe greater buy-in from workers about the governance of the workplace environment if they are involved with the creation of said governance rules. Also, the ongoing feedback from workers about how the code of conduct can be improved allows for ongoing discussions between management and workers. This sense of worth in the workplace environment and having workers' voice be acknowledged can lead to greater worker productivity (see Locke and the two Mexican factories).

The corporation and developing countries

The corporation does not act alone as the case in sweatshops where governments are complacent and do not do anything to stop the corporations from operating on their soil. The impact of the corporation versus the government in developing countries needs to be explored further. What are the conditions that give rise to the sweatshop? Why are individuals so desperate for work that they accept jobs in sweatshops? "The 'moralized' corporation is not necessarily an ethical business resulting from value-driven entrepreneurial spirit or ethical conviction. It is to a large degree due to others applying moral standards to corporate behaviour and forcing corporations to anticipate that."[11] The need to impose morality unto the corporation is hard to resist. However, perhaps the corporation is intended to be void of morals – more a place of neutrality rather than having "bad" morals. While corporations are sometimes expected to "show emotion" after such instances as Rana Plaza, the corporation itself does not necessarily need morals to show emotion.[12] Distancing and the ability to curtail it will help to create a better sense of duty or at least greater respect to those who inhabit host nations when compared with home nations. Perhaps only then will corporations act accordingly when abroad.

Because labour issues are very politically isolating, the government in power may choose to curtail workers' rights in their administration that the next party in power may change. In the case of codes of conduct, there is less chance of codes being changed, as key officials may remain in those positions of power. Also, the potential consumer backlash against changing the codes may be anticipated and fought against. Codes do not have the same strength that hard law offers but are a good alternative for those who are often left out of the political decision-making process. As stated earlier, codes of conduct allow for workers' voices to be included in a way that legislation does not. Workers are often excluded from the governmental realm in that the governing party has never been one focused on labour (the New Democratic Party), and the less powerful members of society such as workers do not have the money to be overly involved with the democratic process.[13]

Codes do not offer the protection that hard law does but may allow coverage for areas that legislation does not – while legislation may govern hours of work, there is room within a code to allow for formation of advantages akin to those gained in a collective agreement. In jurisdictions where union organizing is difficult, there may be ground covered in a code that may not be able to be achieved through hard law. While the future outcome of numerous codes is yet to be realized, the potential of codes is compelling.

Once codes are implemented, the real force and effect comes from having external monitoring agencies that are paid to monitor compliance with the code. Depending on the code itself, the remedy for a breach of the code is usually to try to get the company to fix the problem rather than terminating the

11 Brian Holzer, *Moralizing the Corporation: Transnational Activism and Corporate Accountability* (Northampton: Edward Elgar Publishing Limited, 2010), at 76.

12 Just because Joe Fresh executives show emotion on TV does not mean that the corporation has morals. These two do not have to be connected.

13 This may be a rather sweeping statement but one that is truthful. The poor and overworked are often left out of the political sphere.

contract with the supplier automatically.[14] The nature of the code varies from corporation to corporation, but most identify that suppliers and sub-suppliers must be governed by the code; otherwise, the efficacy is reduced. If the attempt to try to rectify the wrong does not happen, then the relationship may be terminated. As quoted in Chapter 3: "The ultimate sanction against non-compliance is the threat of being de-listed as a supplier. Codes are thus only 'voluntary' to the suppliers in that the alternative is to find new outlets."[15] This is often stipulated in the language of the code itself.

Codes are essential in current society, as the reach of transnational corporations is vast and domestic laws are not able to fully provide a regulatory system that is needed for policing such an organization. Critics may argue that codes allow corporations to get away with behaviour that hard law mechanisms would punish (possibly severely so). The question becomes more akin to what corporations should do when the state fails to act, rather than corporations vying to usurp the power of the state. As articulated by Harry Arthurs, corporate codes may be used to fend off state law because corporations are able to "deflect state law, to create the illusion of law while fending off the reality of regulation."[16] While it may be true that corporations turn to self-regulation as opposed to calling for state regulation, it is not necessarily true that self-regulation is futile. Self-regulation may also be a first step towards increased regulation. As noted by Ed Waitzer and Douglas Sarro, self-regulation includes standard setting, monitoring, and enforcement.[17] Waitzer and Sarro also talk about how managers must be trained about existing codes of conduct so that they understand and are able to keep track of the terms and ensure that the terms of the codes get enforced.

Governance

The intersection between corporate law and labour law is not frequently discussed, as labour law is often left out of corporate law textbooks and classrooms. Labour law may be left out of boardroom discussions, too. Simon Deakin noted that "[w]hile labour law and corporate governance could once have been thought

14 This depends on the terms of the contract itself. The Queen's Code outlines the process by which a supplier can be terminated.

15 Stephanie Barrientos, "Mapping Codes through the Value Chain: From Researcher to Detective" in Rhys Jenkins, Ruth Pearson, & Gill Seyfang (eds.), *Corporate Responsibility and Labour Rights; Codes of Conduct in the Global Economy*, vol. 67 (London: Earthscan Publications Ltd., 2002), at 67.

16 Harry Arthurs, "Profit, Power and Law in the Global Economy" in Wesley Cragg (ed.), *Ethics Codes, Corporations, and the Challenge of Globalization* (Northampton: Edward Elgar Publishing Limited, 2003), at 58.

17 See Ed Waitzer & Douglas Sarro, "Fiduciary Society Unleashed: The Road Ahead for the Financial Sector" online: <http://digitalcommons.osgoode.yorku.ca/olsrps/10/>, at 23.

as discrete area for analysis, it is clear that this is no longer the case."[18] This should not be the case, as the worlds are not so separate and distinct. The intersections and interconnections are becoming more apparent and noteworthy. Professor Peer Zumbansen notes that codes of conduct challenge "traditional understandings of law making, an analysis of voluntary codes of conduct further illuminates the complex nature of the regulated and self-regulating firm."[19] This makes explicit the need for the discussion to be regularly maintained and makes note that the corporation is multifaceted. The corporation is not just being regulated but at the same time is self-regulating. These two somewhat separate issues can happen concurrently. The corporation as a site of power and for power is obvious. The corporation is a site of power in that it wields great power, and it is a site where power can be obtained and controlled. Power as conceived in the Foucault construct can be thought of as

> what makes the domination of a group, a caste, or a class, together with the resistance and revolts which that domination comes up against, a central phenomenon in the history of societies is that they manifest in a massive and universalizing form, at the level of the whole social body, the locking together of power relations with relations of strategy and the results proceeding from their interaction.[20]

Foucault posits that power is legitimated by legal models. But in the world of transnational law, the discussion becomes one of who is the state and what power the state holds in comparison to the corporation.[21] If the power of the corporation overshadows that of the state, then the issue becomes one of why that is the case and how it came to be. Perhaps the discussion can go further into how that power can be reclaimed by the state.[22]

This movement from nation state as the fundamental source of authority has given way to the corporation as a new form of governance. The rise of the corporation and the power and wealth contained therein allowed the corporate form to dominate on the world stage.

18 Simon Deakin as quoted in Peer Zumbansen, "The Parallel Worlds of Corporate Governance and Labor Law" *Indiana Journal of Global Legal Studies* vol 13 (2006) pp. 261–315 at 17.

19 Peer Zumbansen, "The Parallel Worlds of Corporate Governance and Labor Law" *Ind J Glob Leg Stud* vol 13 (2006) pp. 261–315 at 8.

20 Michel Foucault, "The Subject and Power" *Critical Inquiry* vol 8 no 4 (Summer 1982) pp. 777–795 at 795.

21 Michel Foucault, "The Subject and Power" *Critical Inquiry* vol 8 no 4 (Summer 1982) pp. 777–795 at 778: "We had recourse only to ways of thinking about power based on legal models, that is: What legitimates power? Or, we had recourse to ways of thinking about power based on institutional models, that is: What is the state?"

22 It is beyond the scope of this book to pursue answers to such questions, but it is important to acknowledge that these concerns exist.

The rise of international law and transnational governance regimes has also led to the decrease in state power. The ability of goods and services to transcend borders has also allowed for exploitation to carry across borders more easily.

However there is often criticism directed at soft law that it is not effective enough because the penalties for breaches are often not as severe as hard law. I also discussed the UNGC in Chapter 4 and how it has not yet lived up to the potential of creating an international code to which corporations would be able to adhere. The UNGC lacks an enforcement mechanism, so it appears to be quite hollow.

The stretch of laws beyond borders and into the borders of poorer nations may be thought of in a positive manner in that the laws being imported are holding the corporation to the same standards as when it operates on domestic soil. At the same time, it can be viewed as a new mode of invasion – conquering through law.[23] While this could be interpreted as a negative in that the reach of Canadian law should not be allowed to infiltrate other countries, which seems imposing, it could be the case that domestic laws in host nations are being as a result – through this notion of ratcheting labour standards. One way to ratchet is directly through codes of conduct, etc.; but another way to lift standards is indirectly, through the exportation of Canadian laws beyond Canadian borders.

Corporations as citizens

During the course of the book, there is mention of "good corporate citizen" as used by the Supreme Court of Canada and the notion that corporations are citizens and enjoy the rights of citizens accordingly. To delve deeper into this concept, one must ask questions about how the corporation functions as a citizen – do we expect corporations to be active and engaged citizens, or would we expect corporations to be a domicile and blasé citizenry? Corporations have, perhaps unwillingly, been drawn into the political sphere by its decisions to invest, to hire more staff, to move the location of factories and offices, etc. Crane, Matten, and Moon postulate that corporate concerns now include issues such as climate change, poverty, human rights, and social justice.[24] They go on to note that citizens do not merely enjoy rights and freedoms, but also have duties and responsibilities to the society in which they exist.[25] The relationship is symbiotic

23 I created this term to describe a form of imperialism in which a nation is able to export their law to another country through a corporation. This could be a good thing – holding corporations to a standard that would be held to on domestic soil but is often a bad thing.

24 Andrew Crane, Dirk Matten, & Jeremy Moon, *Corporations and Citizenship* (Cambridge: Cambridge University Press, 2008), at 1.

25 Andrew Crane, Dirk Matten, & Jeremy Moon, *Corporations and Citizenship* (Cambridge: Cambridge University Press, 2008), at 7: "By bringing in the Aristotelian assumption about duties of citizenship, to each other and to the polity as a whole, we understand the

and ongoing. Corporations as citizens are also social actors. "[French] argues that the corporation, and not just the people within it, are moral actors and thus the proper subject of ethical evaluations (French 1970). He illustrates this with reference to the evidence that corporations have intentions and thus undertake moral responsibility."[26] The corporation must act ethically as well as the individuals who work within the corporation. If the corporate citizen exists within a democracy, then there is room for the corporation to consolidate power in the form of an oligarchy and can create something close to a monopoly by takeovers and mergers.[27]

Corporations taking over governmental responsibilities in the form of providing clean water for the mining community within which they operate, etc., can be seen as a positive in that people can access clean water, or negative in that the government has failed to provide clean water to its own citizens. Certain roles of the government like the armed forces and police are still hard to be taken over by corporations; however, some corporations hire their own security personnel, such as Shell in Nigeria.[28] Even such core functions of the government can be appropriated by corporations.

Corporations are only able to become involved with governance when government ceases to do so, when government has not yet assumed the task of governing and when it is beyond the reach of the state to govern.[29] The government may be failing when corporate philanthropy is used to improve schools and neighbourhoods in that this may be viewed as stepping into the welfare state.[30] Privatization of public services is another example of the corporation acting when the government decides not to – which is distinct from the government failing to act. When the government has not yet assumed the role then corporations may be forced to start providing health care for their workers and making sure that they receive a living wage. Finally, globalization has made it so that some roles are beyond the role of government. Governments can choose to act to stop climate change but corporations may also have an important role to play in regard to such issues. For example if Shell decided to cut carbon emissions in their worldwide operations this may be more influential than Nigeria forcing Shell to cut carbon emissions – nation state versus the world.

---

citizen's participation in politics not simply as a right to vote or hold office, but also as a contribution to personal development and to societal flourishing."

26 Andrew Crane, Dirk Matten, & Jeremy Moon, *Corporations and Citizenship* (Cambridge: Cambridge University Press, 2008), at 31.

27 I use "close to a monopoly" because the competition bureau and other such organizations are tasked with ensuring that monopolies do not form/exist.

28 Andrew Crane, Dirk Matten, & Jeremy Moon, *Corporations and Citizenship* (Cambridge: Cambridge University Press, 2008), at 5.

29 Andrew Crane, Dirk Matten, & Jeremy Moon, *Corporations and Citizenship* (Cambridge: Cambridge University Press, 2008), at 64.

30 Andrew Crane, Dirk Matten, & Jeremy Moon, *Corporations and Citizenship* (Cambridge: Cambridge University Press, 2008), at 65.

The future for workers' rights

While I argue that codes of conduct are the best way forward for workers, critics of CSR may argue that codes are not the best way to secure or increase the rights of workers. With the rise of capitalism and what may be termed "corporatism," workers must be willing to acknowledge that power and the ability to gain strength in their collective ability allows for speaking truth to power. Only through engaging with corporations will workers be able to forge ahead. The labour movement in many forms has accepted this new mode and has adapted as a result.[31] For workers to have a seat at the table like in the German model may be just one option, and other options may prove useful to other workplaces; no one solution will work in every single workplace. If workers are given increased autonomy and voice about their workplaces, then they would be able to choose which model works for their individual workplace.

Bibliography for Chapter 5

Secondary sources

Books

Crane, Andrew, Dirk Matten, & Jeremy Moon, *Corporations and Citizenship* (Cambridge: Cambridge University Press, 2008).

Ellis, Mark, *Fiduciary Duties in Canada, Looseleaf* (Toronto: Carswell, 2011).

Holzer, Brian, *Moralizing the Corporation: Transnational Activism and Corporate Accountability* (Northampton: Edward Elgar Publishing Limited, 2010).

Book chapters

Arthurs, Harry, "Profit, Power and Law in the Global Economy" in Wesley Cragg, ed., *Ethics Codes, Corporations, and the Challenge of Globalization* (Northampton: Edward Elgar Publishing Limited, 2003).

Barrientos, Stephanie, "Mapping Codes Through the Value Chain: From Researcher to Detective" in Rhys Jenkins, Ruth Pearson, & Gill Seyfang, eds., *Corporate Responsibility and Labour Rights: Codes of Conduct in the Global Economy*, 67 (London: Earthscan Publications Ltd., 2002).

Articles

Foucault, Michel, "The Subject and Power" *Critical Inquiry* vol 8 no 4 (Summer 1982) pp. 777–795.

O'Reilly, Jane, "Is Negative Attention Better Than No Attention? The Comparative Effects of Ostracism and Harassment at Work," online: <http://pubsonline.informs.org/doi/abs/10.1287/orsc.2014.0900>.

31 See the Framework of Fairness.

Sukdeo, Vanisha H., "Transnational Governance Models: Codes of Conduct and Monitoring Agencies as Tools to Increase Workers' Rights" *German Law Journal* vol 13 no 12 (2012) pp. 1559–1570.

Waitzer, Edward & Douglas Sarro, "Fiduciary Society Unleashed: The Road Ahead for the Financial Sector" at 23, online: <http://digitalcommons.osgoode.yorku.ca/olsrps/10/>.

Zumbansen, Peer, "The Parallel Worlds of Corporate Governance and Labor Law" *Indiana Journal of Global Legal Studies* vol 13 (2006) pp. 261–315.

Websites

Larry Cata Backer blog post on September 21, 2013, online: <http://lcbackerblog.blogspot.ca/2013/09/changing-corporate-behavior-through.html>.

Index

www.ingramcontent.com/pod-product-compliance
Ingram Content Group UK Ltd.
Pitfield, Milton Keynes, MK11 3LW, UK
UKHW011019180926
475701UK00004B/824
9781032241012